Living before you Die

FRED BROWN

SCM PRESS LTD

334 00919 7

First published 1973
by SCM Press Ltd
56 Bloomsbury Street, London

© SCM Press Ltd 1973

Printed in Great Britain by
Cox & Wyman Ltd
London, Fakenham and Reading

Living before you Die

Contents

Introduction   7

1 Committed Unbelievers   11

2 Doctrines were made for Men   27

3 The Touchstone of Truth   38

4 Religious Experience without Belief in God   59

5 Worship of God is the Celebration of Man   77

6 The Saviourhood of Christ   94

7 Life is Resurrection   114

Introduction

This book, which has grown out of my research at Queen's College, Birmingham, is about religious experience both inside and, more particularly, outside the institution of the church. After conversations with all kinds of individuals, young and old, I am convinced that a silent revolution is taking place in the way people think about God and organized religion generally. Time and again, most of all in talking with younger people, I get the impression that while the institutional church continues to lose her appeal the very opposite is true of the reality for which the church stands. Paradoxically the subject, not of God, but of religious experience, commands widespread and, I believe, growing interest. It is increasingly taken for granted that belief in God as traditionally outlined is not essential for transcendental explorations, and this assumption, I have discovered, is not restricted to non-churchgoers.

Thomas Merton, a Trappist monk, summarized one aspect of the situation, and shared an interesting personal sequel of no small significance, in his book *Contemplation in a World of Action*:

> In actual fact, the gift of supernatural faith does not in any way depend on whether or not man is naturally disposed to accept easily a congenial concept of God. It is after all quite common for us in dechristianized cultures to encounter

7

persons who have never had a serious thought about God, one way or the other, and who have suddenly been struck, in the most unaccountable manner, by the light of faith. It is customary among pious people to imagine that this is always a beautiful and consoling experience. It is sometimes frightening. You fortunate believer! You do not know the confusion, the bewilderment and the suffering of an atheist who has suddenly, without any apparent human intervention, been literally overwhelmed by the reality of God, and who does not know what to do. Surrounded by friends who can only mock him, if he reveals his trouble, unable to pray, unable to trust himself to the Church of which he is highly suspicious, he is in a state of heartbreaking anguish. Perhaps it may be true that he is a 'naturally Christian soul'. God does not present Himself to him in a clear and comforting concept, but as a completely disconcerting and inexplicable reality, making a demand for total commitment and trust. His anguish is all the greater, but his faith is no less real. And he turns, instinctively, to the contemplatives who, he believes, are men of prayer and know the ways of God. But when he comes to us, in profound distress, we become aware of our own insufficiency; and we carefully weigh any words we may say, knowing that they must not be sentimental or complacent or merely formal. The writer of these lines recently had one of many such experiences: and he knows that it is utterly false to claim that 'modern man is incapable of feeling the need for God; or responding to His presence'.[1]

I also am sure about the falsehood of the claim that modern man is incapable of feeling the need for God. At the same time – and this is where so much confusion arises – modern man's concept of God and spirituality is anything but orthodox, and his response to God's presence is understood in strictly non-religious terms. Another fundamental difference is that much of the scepticism often associated with religious belief has been undermined by the questions which modern man now feels compelled to ask about what it means to be human, to be a whole person. Not so long ago, notably in intellectual circles, it was confidently assumed that religion generally and institutional religion in particular were evidences of man's immaturity and inability to cope. Only when the need for such supports were outgrown would man be free to fulfil his own potential, to discover, in fact, the infinite possibilities of his own nature. Until then, religion and all its conventional trimmings were hindrances for the strong and unfortunate crutches for the weak.

Such bold verbosity is now largely out of fashion. Indeed, one of the few institutions losing its membership faster than the church is the British Humanist Association. It need hardly be said that this is not explained by humanists being converted to conventional religion. They are usually no less committed to their humanistic ideas, but such a commitment, many of them are apparently now perceiving, is not necessarily incompatible with the recognition that the drive to transcendence within man points to an essential dimension of human experience about which institutional religion bears witness and also gently insists is the key to fulness of life NOW.

In what follows, I have tried, within the space at my disposal, to face some of the implications of this development; to face them primarily by asking big questions and offering, not answers, but comments which I hope will evoke open and frank discussion. For this, it seems to me, is the great need of the moment. The institutional church is in ferment, indicative surely of life not death, but two possibilities concern me: I fear that institutional religion will become more reactionary as its numerical strength continues to diminish; and that complex questions will be silenced as over-simple answers labelled orthodoxy are substituted for honest doubt and open-ended enquiry.

If my book helps in any small way to overcome such self-defeating trends I shall be more than satisfied.

NOTE

1. Thomas Merton, *Contemplation in a World of Action,* Allen & Unwin 1970, pp.175–6.

Committed Unbelievers

The youthful visitor was obviously impressed beyond her expectations. Looking around the dining hall at Queen's College, Birmingham, her eyes widening with growing incredulity, she remarked: 'Who would think that they're training to be parsons?' *They* were some eighty men, the vast majority under thirty years of age, who reflected, occasionally in extreme form, the non-conformist gaiety of modern society. If you want to argue that non-conformist gaiety is not characteristic of contemporary society I can only reply that the part of it I know best, centring on Carnaby Street in London's West End, is decidedly non-conformist and addicted to gaiety. But let us not get side-tracked. The only point I want to make is that this group of potential parsons hardly represented the image usually associated with the church.

Some of them, it is true, wore conventional clothes, like suits and ties, but most of them – at least this was the youthful visitor's impression – looked like fully paid-up members of the gayest of with-it clubs. Despite the occasional short back and sides, their hair seemed inordinately long, sometimes reaching the shoulders, if not the shoulder-blades. And the world being what it is, they looked indecently happy. Laughter resounded almost non-stop, with occasional explosions of mirth that made London Palladium audiences at their merriest sound like a collection of professional mourners.

I was not surprised at the visitor's reaction. Anything less like a theological college would be hard to imagine. Yet Queen's is in the parson-growing business in a big way already and all the indications suggest that, unlike some similar institutions, its future is not behind it; decidedly not. This ecumenical community has developed out of the amalgamation of the original Queen's, an Anglican establishment, and Handsworth College, which was Methodist. The two traditions have contributed to the creative tension that pulsates at the heart of their united life, but there is, I think, far more to it than that. There is tension, and plenty of it, as the twice-weekly open community meetings reveal, but it tends to be creative because of the nature of its motivation. Inevitably there is sometimes pettiness and the sort of discussion that generates more heat than light. It is not unknown for disagreements to arise, in which case democratic methods do not always resolve smouldering resentments, but generally speaking the life of the community is positive and progressive.

The reason – and I must be careful not to appear to claim more than I intend – is the common commitment and faith; faith as distinct from belief. For to say that there is no common theology is a polite understatement. The vast majority of men, it is true, are orthodox in their beliefs, allowing of course that orthodoxy these days permits a measure of elasticity previously unknown in the church, but a minority whose influence and perhaps significance outweigh their numbers are decidedly unorthodox. They are confused, yet sure. They despair of the church, yet choose deliberately to stay in it. They find it increasingly difficult to say what they believe, yet are certain of nothing more than that they *do* believe. They know that they have a vocation, yet do not exactly understand what that vocation is. They zealously train for the ministry, yet often wonder, feeling as they do, why they bother.

Now the confusion which they epitomize is, to varying degrees, characteristic of the whole community at Queen's. But paradoxically it represents rather than denies conviction, real conviction that is, the type that drives a man on in spite of himself; causes him 'to set his face to Jerusalem' with singleness of aim. There are men, of course, who are wholly happy with traditional theology and methods of worship. They revel in the life of the church and want nothing more than to safeguard the *status quo*. It is not necessarily that they are either unaware of what is happening in the world or indifferent about bridging the widening gulf between the church and the multitudes at present beyond her influence, but they genuinely believe that the best and indeed the only way to meet the challenge confronting Christianity in secular society is for the church to stand immovable: be true to her time-honoured words and ways, and refuse resolutely to make any concessions to the clamour for change. They are not typical, but they are, I believe, an essential element in the life of any theological college which is concerned to be a community of enterprise. However, usually beyond their knowing, they actually add to the general confusion, for their insistence upon unyielding obedience to the present – meaning the past – way of doing things, notably in terms of worship, leads inescapably to confusion worse confounded for individuals not on their ecclesiastical wavelength.

The answer, or a major part of it – and this is where Queen's scores full marks – is to admit the confusion and perceive that contrary to possible superficial impressions, it does not represent denial of the essential Christian spirit or witness. Too often in the church we identify confusion with *un*faith, as though to be unsure of traditional definitions was the same as rejecting the reality within those definitions. We appear to imagine that orderliness is the guarantee of truth, not realizing that order is sometimes the enemy of needed exploration. For the guidelines of order, particularly when given a divine mandate, so easily pre-determine conclusions which not only stifle the spirit but evolve into systems of rigid orthodoxy. The community at Queen's College *is* confused because it is made up of potential priests and ministers who refuse to hide their confusion under a camouflage of skilful verbiage. They admit their confusion without glorying in it. It is the confusion of a search for truth which is only possible because truth has already been found.

Let me be more personal. Here is a university graduate in the final stages of his preparation for ordination. He is doing a second degree course and is keenly anticipating his wider ministry. His sense of vocation, like his commitment to the church, is beyond doubt. Yet he finds belief in God as traditionally taught by institutional Christianity virtually impossible. As a boy he did so once believe, but recent years have seen a transformation in his thinking about most things, not least his understanding of theology. For him the word G–O–D creates only problems and what at times looks like insuperable difficulties. Nevertheless he wants to be a Christian minister and believes that he has a faith worth sharing, one which in functional terms detracts not at all from the essential message of the Christian church. The years might well change his mind, causing him to see that the word G–O–D, despite the wide divergence of meaning it conveys even within the church, is still indispensable to symbolize man's understanding of ultimate reality, but meanwhile he, like a handful of fellow-students who share his views, believes in the church and wants to support her ministry in the world.

This ambivalent attitude is perhaps most vividly focused in the college chapel. On weekdays four services are held daily; attendance is voluntary and the services themselves are conducted in the main by the students. On Sunday the entire community comes together to celebrate the eucharist, alternating between Anglican and Methodist celebrants and liturgical forms. Such openness means that rigidity of any kind is out of the question. The riches of traditional worship are safeguarded, obviously to varying degrees of satisfaction according to personal preference, but there is unlimited scope for experiment, and this results in all manner of bold ventures to relate worship to central concerns of contemporary life. Some of these occasions have proved to be unforgettably helpful; others have been gratefully forgotten. Beyond doubt, however, the opportunities for this variety of worship are unique in the experience of every student and add immeasurably to his understanding of the possibilities within the existing institutional church.

Nevertheless it must be admitted that for a sizeable minority of the clergy-to-be perhaps no aspect of the community's life is less satisfactory than the activities within the chapel. In itself, this illustrates the paradox at the heart of the commitment of these men to the church, for if they find such a rich choice of approaches to worship still little more than boring – their favourite word to sum up their feelings – what chance is there that they will ever feel at home in the church?

I ask the question in that form not to imply that they should fulfil their vocation elsewhere, but rather to underline the dilemma that confronts them and, I believe, a growing number of churchmen generally. My concern – let it be clearly understood – is not to point out how unsuited such potential parsons are for the church's ministry. I happen to think the very opposite. No, I simply want to make the point that the men themselves, despite their difficulties with traditional theology, still want to remain within and work for the church. Why? Because, as they have explained to me, one after another, whatever their sometimes near despair with the institutional church, they *know* that what the church represents is the key to the whole of life.

They do not want to argue about theological definitions or insist upon any stereotype of worship. Such considerations, ironically enough, are to them of secondary importance. But they want to make an emphasis: they want to stand for the approach to life which they see exemplified in Jesus of Nazareth but find increasingly difficult to talk about. I believe that their witness – and no other word will do – is profoundly significant for the whole church and pregnant with meaning. Indeed, I wonder whether these young radicals are not saying something of significance about a world of organized religion, sick of materialism, disillusioned by technology, and disenchanted by the reputed affluence of western society. They know that life has more to it than *that*.

The question is not whether the church thinks these potential parsons fit to share her ministry, but whether she is prepared to listen seriously, as distinct from patronizingly, to what they are trying to say or even to what God is possibly trying to say through them. If so, what is the message? An essential part of it is perhaps related to an insight shared by Erich Fromm in a book first published nearly a quarter of a century ago:

Unfortunately the discussion centred around religion since the days of the Enlightenment has been largely concerned with the affirmation or negation of a belief in God rather than with the affirmation or negation of certain human attitudes. 'Do you believe in the existence of God?' has been made the crucial question of religionists and the denial of God has been the position chosen by those fighting the church. It is easy to see that many who profess the belief in God are in their human attitude idol worshippers or men without faith, while some of the most ardent 'atheists', devoting their lives to the betterment of mankind, to deeds of brotherliness and love, have exhibited faith and a profoundly religious attitude.

Centring the religious discussion on the acceptance or denial of the symbol God blocks the understanding of the religious problem as a human problem and prevents the development of that human attitude which can be called religious in a humanistic sense.[1]

What *is* belief in God: a confession of faith, the sort that gives mental assent to religious dogma, or a wondering openness to life? Put otherwise, is belief in God a matter of subscribing to religious statements or living religiously? Clearly the two are frequently related, the one sometimes but not always inspiring the other. Increasingly these days individuals tend to dismiss the idea of God as taught by the institutional church, but they function religiously, adopting an attitude to life reminiscent of the spirit of Jesus of Nazareth. I am not referring to men and women in general. Unhappily the decline in institutional religion is not matched conversely by an increase in the number of people who live religiously, but there are individuals, significantly both inside and outside the church, who find belief in God either impossible or meaningless and yet who live as though they do believe. Unlike the religious hypocrite who professes with his lips what he denies with his life, they affirm with their lives what they deny with their lips. Are they to be called disbelievers and made to feel that they have no place – or only a begrudged one – in the church? Most of them, of course, *are* outside the church and hardly give the impression of wanting to get inside; but there are some who feel at home in the church and genuinely want to share her life and witness. As far as the handful of theological students I have mentioned are concerned they find orthodox belief in God both impossible and unnecessary as they translate their commitment to Jesus of Nazareth into a way of life; and clearly this makes no perceptible difference to their ability to function as real persons or reflects adversely on the spirit of their dedication to Christian service. One of them justified his continuance in the church, despite his non-theistic belief, by saying that he personally found wholeness within the church and knew of no better agency by which either to nourish his own experiential faith or share it with others. The central question, it seems to me, is not whether such believers – or disbelievers, according to your point of view – have a place in the church, but whether the cultivation of their religious attitude to life is not a forceful reminder that this in essence is what belief in God is all about anyway!

For too long the church has made God the subject of theological debate, as though if she could persuade people to believe in him, give mental assent to the claim that he *is* as taught by institutional religion, then they could be placed among the number of believers and qualify for full membership. Undoubtedly this has proved to be a valid way for some individuals, as they themselves gratefully testify. But is it the only way? Many responsible churchmen are moving from the exclusive claims once made by the church, that she alone is the custodian of the whole truth about God through the revelation of Jesus Christ, for they see evidence that other world religions largely complement rather than contradict the insights of Christianity. What is more to the point, they recognize that any revelation of God is made to one or more people; and they wonder to which person or persons the *whole* truth about God has been made known. The very idea is clearly self-contradictory and finally ludicrous. However, all this, though significant, is not the main point at issue. The real question, I believe, belongs to another area altogether.

We can best approach it – indeed, the only reliable approach we can make – is from the end of human experience. If we do this we are immediately faced with the reality of people who reject religion but live religiously. To be more precise, we have the conundrum of young men who do not believe in God wanting to enter the ministry of the Christian church and living as though 'God' was the most real factor in their experience. To ignore that situation or attempt to rationalize it, which is a favourite dodge of ecclesiastical peace-makers, is to turn away from life as some people know it and possibly to turn away from the truth that makes men free. It could be argued, I realize, that this is merely a phase through which adolescent minds are passing and that sooner or later the individuals concerned will grow into orthodox belief. The problem, for purveyors of this point of view, is that not all the godless churchmen and rejecters of institutional religion who live religiously are young; they represent every age group.

But let us stick to our potential parsons as typifying the sort of religious outlook I have in mind. What are we to make of them? It seems to me that the more pertinent question is, what are they to make of us – *us* meaning believers in God as taught by the church. For at the moment we tend to deny the validity of their spiritual experience in the name of defending our supposedly orthodox point of view. Or perhaps we do not deny it entirely. Rather we dogmatize that only when that experience is articulated in harmony with the church's representations of truth can it be considered authentic, a focal point beyond doubt of God's action. But surely theology has to be fashioned by life, not life somehow made to corroborate theology! At the moment the reverse is the case. Institutional religion dogmatizes about the truth, insisting with varying degrees of tolerance that human experience is good and proper only to the extent that it confirms the imperatives of orthodox teaching.

The results of this approach illustrate that the church has sometimes proved to be opposed to life. She has imposed – at times ruthlessly – concepts of belief and behaviour which in retrospect are recognized as alien to the very spirit of the good news she was commissioned to declare. All too apparently Christian liberty was understood in terms of rigid obedience to accredited doctrines, for the church, it was believed, alone possessed detailed knowledge of the mind of God and therefore of the only way man must live to please him. Seeing that nothing else in life or death was adjudged to be more important, no measures were thought to be unlawful if they served the purpose of *persuading* a heretic or a believer under suspicion to mend his ways. When human experience in terms of Christian living pointed to the error of this uncompromising policy, indicating that the teaching of the church, far from being on the side of life, was entrenched against it, human experience was always dismissed as dangerously misleading and probably as evidence of secret indulgence. You see, the assumption was unfailingly made that the theology of organized religion – the current theology – was the one touchstone against which *truth* must be tested. It was unthinkable to the point of blasphemy that human experience should re-write theology, for such a procedure, it was believed, would make little more than a convenience of the absolute truth revealed by God to his infallible church. Such ideas in those days were understandable and from some standpoints excusable. The trouble is that they tend to linger, being mistaken still for symptoms of holy zeal and defence of truth.

Nevertheless, it is beyond doubt that increasingly men are recognizing that theology is essentially about *life* or about nothing worth a second thought. Unless God *is* dead, no theological system is sacrosanct or has the final word about anything. One of the inevitable consequences of this comparatively new approach of revealed religion is the awareness that unless theology impinges on life at the points of men's greatest concerns it is worse than useless. In other words, only when theology is related to human creativity is it more than self-indulgent mental gymnastics. It is now perceived as never before that traditionally theologians – and their devoutness is not in question – have weaved patterns of speculative theistic thought and genuinely believed that their dogmatic conclusions represented 'revealed truth'. Unhappily such immodesty was encouraged by the institution to which they belonged and their teaching, some of it now seen as blatantly unChristian, given official sanction in the name of God. But most Christian thinkers these days have no doubt that he is not so easily wrapped up in our neat and tidy theological parcels. Indeed, a few of them appear to have gone to the other extreme and insist that we can know next to nothing about the mysteries of the Godhead, always supposing that there is a Godhead we can know next to nothing about. Most theologians, however, are less abject in their humility. They simply acknowledge that we know far less about ultimate reality than was once confidently supposed.

What unites and at times excites them is the insight that theology is about life, related to the profundities of human experience. After all, what is the use of believing that, for instance, Jesus Christ died for our sins unless such words represent experiential knowledge? Yet there are still earnest proselytizers who imagine that they have won a convert once he has been persuaded to say that he believes this or that. The problem is that so often the words remain nothing more than a sort of metaphysical formula, one that admittedly initiates some people into a desired spiritual experience, but certainly not everybody. Most people remain only baffled and bewildered, mouthing words that express not ecstasy but exasperation.

Again, what does it mean to say that I believe in the trinity? The answer of classical theology is clear-cut, but of what am I really deprived if I find such thought-patterns incredible? There are devout Christians, I realize, who claim that I am deprived of a great deal, and I respect their view. I respect it, but I do not understand it. For there are equally devout Christians, members of the church and eagerly involved in her life and witness, who tell me that belief in the trinity for them only creates problems, and is neither here nor there. It makes no difference at all, they say, to the way a man lives.

The same applies, it seems, to so many other supposedly indispensable articles of faith. To be a Christian – that is, the most authentic type of Christian – you must, says the Roman Catholic Church, believe this and this and this; the list seems forbidding and endless. But when I consult members of other denominations I find that their lists vary considerably. Some of them insist that I *must* believe in the virgin birth; others tell me that such belief is optional, quite unnecessary to the essential Christian gospel. They all strike me as intelligent, responsible people, often winsome in their personalities, and certainly indistinguishable from the standpoint of whether or not they believe that Jesus of Nazareth was born of a virgin.

In like manner I find myself confronted by a number of alternative formulations of belief, some of them deemed essential, though they almost never agree from list to list. A few of them make claims which if valid put many churchmen beyond the pale. All this indicates to what extent theology is often unrelated to life, for clearly it makes no apparent difference whether I believe many of the traditional doctrines or not. Yet surely it should if they represent truth crucial to man's salvation! Theoretically it should matter, but experientially it does not. So why not drop the pretence and make it abundantly clear that in the realm of metaphysics one man's truth is another man's irrelevance; or rather the articulation of one man's truth is another man's irrelevance? For it is surely conceivable that though men differ about doctrinal definitions and other symbols of faith they are united fundamentally in their experiential knowledge of the reality to which Christians of all persuasions unanimously point.

Let me make myself clear. I am not arguing that Christian doctrine is unimportant. My only concern is to illustrate that

22

if on the churches' own admission many of the traditional doctrines are now optional, offered on a take-it-or-leave-it basis, there is no reason to perpetuate the myth that the teaching of the church, the *whole* teaching, is either essential to faith or related inseparably to the warp and woof of life. Looked at from another standpoint, this means that to believe – genuinely to give mental assent to – the whole teaching of the church is no guarantee of possessing experiential knowledge of the truth to which she bears witness. And it is the experiential knowledge of the truth some men call God with which we are confronted.

Again I stress the experiential for the same reason; it is obviously possible for people to say that they believe the Christian doctrine of God and be capable of skilful argument in its defence, yet still function as practical atheists. The reason is not hypocrisy or any other form of pretentiousness. It is simply that the belief is no more than a mental concept, like the right answer to a theoretical problem. It represents a formulation of words which, true or false, have no discernible practical application. The belief exists in a kind of vacuum, unrelated to the real issues of life.

There are people, too, who believe in God as a funk hole from the harshness or feared harshness of their lot. They believe, sometimes to the point of bigotry, and in consequence their favourite pastime is unconscious devout self-centredness. Asked if they believe in God, they reply with the disdain of people who are offended that such a question is thought necessary. Of course they believe! Significantly, the reaction of a growing number of people is simply: 'So what!'

With this in mind, I want to ask if it is possible that in pushing belief in God as the cardinal article of faith – that is, belief in God as usually understood – the church is not making it more difficult for many individuals to come to terms with her message? This is notably true, I believe, at this particular point in history, for when the church talks about God she speaks as never before in many voices and appears to mean different things. The situation is not helped by responsible churchmen who, knowing that this is the case, and wishing for themselves that a greater degree of clarity were possible, continue nevertheless to talk about God as though the one word carried singleness of meaning. The reason, needless to say, is not any wish to deceive or to over-simplify a complex area of man's search for understanding. Indeed, to their credit, some church leaders have publicly expressed the wish that the word God could be dropped, for a decade or two at least, and a more meaningful substitute found, but at the same time they have acknowledged that probably the three letters G–O–D will continue to prove themselves irreplaceable. The reasons for this are straightforward enough, being bedded, among other things, in man's sense of history, but they do not alter the fact that the word God means different things to different people sometimes to the degree of unifying contradictory concepts.

There are pious voices which seek to silence this babel of conviction by calling people back to a biblical understanding of God, meaning *their* particular point of view, but more sensitive churchmen, aware of the ferment within the church and not afraid to add to it themselves by occasionally thinking aloud, cheerfully recognize that the word God is really no longer adequate to represent a growing multiplicity of meaning. The trouble is, as I have said, no other word will do.

Now this creates real problems when people say that they no longer believe in God and yet clearly – sometimes on their own insistence – believe in the interpretation of life for which the church stands. I believe that this double-bind situation is already not uncommon and will become more prevalent within the next twenty-five years at most. The word God is discredited with a lot of people because the meanings traditionally associated with it are no longer acceptable, even intelligible – which explains why people are inclined to *say* that they disbelieve in God – but they continue in the church because predominantly they still believe that Christianity, speaking of the dimension of life which transcends time and space, the dimension of human experience which is non-rational as distinct from irrational, represents a way of life which, they feel in their very bones, leads to wholeness. They find that Jesus of Nazareth – the symbolic meaning of his birth, life, death and resurrection – helps them to understand and interpret what life fundamentally is all about, whereas God-talk of the traditional variety erects barriers and cuts them off from reality.

This being the case – and remember that we are talking about real people, not figments of our theological imagination – we are bound to ask to what degree individuals who do not believe in God as conventionally identified are hindered in their experiential knowledge of the essential truth to which Jesus of Nazareth testified? What I am really asking is this: what in real-life terms do persons who believe in God possess which is denied to disbelievers who nevertheless live religiously? Is it something distinctive and exclusive to orthodox belief? I readily admit the difficulty of such questions, but if they are related to vital issues, as some theists adamantly insist, then some sort of answer should clearly emerge. All I can say is that in my experience this is not the case. What usually happens is that the discussion centres upon patterns of thought called theology; and even when a measure of agreement is reached about meanings, the basic area of concern remains as obscure as ever. In fact, I have noticed that the outcome of such discussion is more dependent upon the respective participant's facility with words than any change of mind, one way or the other. Individuals lose arguments, possibly silenced by skilful eloquence rather than irresistible logic, but they maintain their position tenaciously, convinced that far more than verbal surrender is at stake.

What I am trying to say is that theology remains speculative and theoretical unless considered in real-life terms, and that, when so considered, major points of theological controversy are seen for what they are – academic exercises removed from the actualities of life. Understandably, some professional theologians disagree, but they have surely only to ask themselves why the vast majority of books on theology are unread by the vast majority of people to get the point that most people think of them as wholly irrelevant.

The majority of believers, of those I have questioned unhurriedly, use the word God to symbolize a way of life. Almost invariably, when pressed to say more precisely what they mean by God, they settle for a total view of life that expresses the spirit and outlook of Jesus of Nazareth. The crucial question for them, as Erich Fromm suggested, is not whether they say that they believe or disbelieve in God, but whether their attitude to life is truly religious; that is, one of wondering openness and faith and hope. As we shall see, religious experience is not belief-dependent, at least not to the degree we have usually taken for granted.

NOTE

1. Erich Fromm, *Psychoanalysis and Religion*, Yale University Press 1950; Bantam Books 1970, pp.109–10.

2

Doctrines were made for Men

When a man says he believes in God or claims that Christianity is true, he is making a statement of faith not merely about one creed in preference to another or indeed about theological definitions of whatever kind. Essentially he is saying that he finds the Christian faith thoroughly reliable in the sense that he finds it trustworthy. He is prepared to bet his life on it, whatever the arguments about the church's doctrinal and moral teaching. Truth about God or ultimate reality is not, he knows, a dogmatic formulation of words. That is to objectify it in a way that leads to claims of infallibility – putting people who disagree somehow outside the inner circle with the corollary that the believers inside know better or more than everybody else.

Fundamentally, truth about God is essentially personal; about personal values and relationships. And it follows from this that the question 'Is it true?' should be 'Is it reliable?', for the sort of truth we are considering is about what we know to be utterly trustworthy and dependable. We know, if you like, as much with our hearts as our heads; the two are not incompatible, least of all contradictory, but in this area of truth the knowing of the heart transcends the knowledge of the head, or at least the way that knowledge is articulated.

At the risk of belabouring the point, I want to consider

this situation in terms of the local church. Some of the members reflect the spirit of Jesus of Nazareth and humbly testify that, if this is so, it is because of their Christian faith. They believe the doctrines, and their way of life seems the spontaneous outcome. But with other members it is different. They, too, believe the doctrines and are no less zealous in their churchgoing, yet they seem petty, fault-finding, and judgmental. Now I am not wanting to compare the two – or twenty – types of believers. They are different, I realize, for all sorts of reasons, but the one thing they have in common is their beliefs. They claim to believe the *truth* of Christianity which they define and often teach in precisely the same terms. Is the explanation simply that they come from various backgrounds and represent a wide variation of personality? Is it really as straightforward as that? I remain unconvinced.

In the first place Christianity is usually regarded as a religion of power. To accept its teaching is, preachers insist, to release into one's life the power to change, if not into a saint overnight (though this claim is still often made), at least into a person who is moving in the direction of sanctity or wholeness. The fact is, however, that some life-long believers of conviction remain caricatures of the image we usually associate with the authentic Christian. Is their belief, orthodox to the letter, so powerless to change them?

The obvious retort is to suggest that people who live the Christian life are the *true* believers, whereas those who do not, despite the fervour of their declared orthodoxy, are insincere or self-deceived. Allowing for possible seeds of truth in such a comment, I find it both obnoxious and unhelpful. In any case, who is to decide which of us is insincere or self-deceived? We cannot possibly know, if only because such judgment belongs to the realm of motivation of which God alone is fully informed. It could be that the people we think are sub-standard are battling with secret problems and proving in unsuspected ways the validity of their religious beliefs. It could be. On the other hand, it is true that the only way to assess the relation, if any, between religious belief and behaviour is to look at the lives of religious (and non-religious) people. When we do so, without censoriousness or other forms of pomposity, we are bound to conclude that in many cases the relation appears to be tenuous.

There is, of course, another explanation, one that leads to the opposite conclusion. It is that the relation between belief and behaviour in all circumstances is so strong that sub-Christian living, whatever the claims to orthodoxy and no matter how strong the commitment to supposed Christian truth, simply reveals secret wrong thinking about God and ultimate concerns generally. What could be more obvious, a perfect summing up of the situation! Unfortunately, as is often the case, such rationalization is too easy and finally leads nowhere. For in terms of how people actually live, religious belief, orthodox or otherwise, or no religious belief at all appears often to make little difference.

From this standpoint, the standpoint of living experience, the crucial factor in deciding what is truth becomes self-evident: the major criterion of judgment is what belief does in the life of the believer. This remembered, the conclusion to which we are driven is heavily underlined – that people whose way of life appears to be virtually identical sometimes have religious beliefs which are mutually denying and sometimes they have no conscious religious beliefs at all. What I am asking basically is the extent to which religious truth can be judged in an objective sense. It seems to me that merely to ask the question is to receive an unambiguous answer. For surely there is no way of knowing, not to the extent of being absolutely sure, that beliefs about God and metaphysical beliefs generally represent the exact truth or even point beyond doubt in that direction. There is often substantial evidence to support statements of faith, but no final objective proof of infallibility.

The concept of the infallible church evolved almost inevitably from the conviction that the power of reality behind the universe – God – had revealed himself to men or more particularly to a select group of men. They were truly in the know, which meant that they alone could speak authoritatively about the truth of God and his will for mankind. The sources of revelation were Jesus of Nazareth, the key, they believed, to their whole understanding of God; the Holy Spirit, the Spirit of Truth, who guarded them from error; the scriptures which pointed to, and told the story of, the word made flesh; and ongoing history, some of the lessons of which contributed to what was called tradition.

By such means the accredited leaders of the church were guided into all truth, and kept informed of God's will and purpose for the whole world. There was only one way of salvation, the way revealed to, and taught by, the Christian church. Salvation was identified with church membership, an identification which sometimes expressed itself in inhuman policies. The threat of excommunication became a tyranny, for men believed that to be excommunicated was to be condemned to eternal damnation. And heretics, for the supposed good of their souls, were persecuted with devout brutality to encourage their recantations and thereby restore them to a right relationship with God, the only thing that finally mattered and the justification, therefore, for reigns of terror in the name of truth.

The infallibility of the ecclesiastical hierarchy, epitomized by the Pope, was largely taken for granted until the middle of the nineteenth century, when God's Vicar, exasperated by what he felt was the unco-operative – indeed blasphemous – attitude of the Italian government over a question of Papal States, demanded a definition of infallibility and a dogmatic statement that the papacy was infallible, at least on selected occasions. The statement was made on 18 July 1870, and incorporated the claim that the church's teaching was made known to be infallible in three distinct ways. First, when the Pope spoke *ex cathedra*, meaning those occasions when the Roman pontiff, exercising the office of a pastor and teacher of all Christians, defined with his supreme apostolic authority a doctrine concerning faith or morals to be held by the universal church, through the divine assistance promised to him in blessed Peter. Second, when the ecumenical council gave a binding definition of doctrine on faith and morals. And third, when the totality of bishops throughout the world, together with the Pope, agreed on a truth of faith or morals held by all the faithful.

It will readily be seen that these mediums of papal infallibility sometimes contradict each other or cancel each other out. For instance, the present Pope, ignoring the majority report of the council he had set up to look into the matter, recently affirmed the church's traditional teaching on conception control, teaching about which the totality of bishops throughout the world are openly divided. Yet their unanimous agreement is otherwise made the basis of claims of infallibility. Clearly some mediums of infallibility are more infallible than others!

However, my main purpose is not to analyse the authoritarianism of the Roman Catholic Church so much as to illustrate how that authoritarianism is now operating in certain parts of the world and the nature of the difficulties it creates for a growing number of committed Christians. They know that the church no longer speaks with one voice; that statements from within the hierarchy itself are often contradictory and represent at best compromise solutions to complexities about which agreement appears impossible. In such circumstances an authoritative statement by the Pope, uttered *ex cathedra* or not, far from silencing dissenting voices, only brings into sharper focus the fundamental differences that characterize almost every aspect of ecclesiastical and theological discussion. Church leaders either fail to perceive or conveniently forget to remember that there is no such thing as the direct revelation of God. Rather, God reveals himself to this person or that group of persons, and then the articulation or interpretation of the revelation, if such it is, is attempted. 'There is no such thing as revealed truth,' said the late Archbishop William Temple. 'There are truths of revelation, that is to say, propositions which express the results of correct thinking concerning revelation; but they are not themselves directly revealed.'[1] The trouble is that the supposed 'correct thinking' almost never wins universal assent, notably among the church's official thinkers, sometimes called theologians. It seems that one man's orthodoxy is another man's heresy; and the two roles change with bewildering rapidity these days.

In an attempt to extricate the church from the pit of infallibility she has dug for herself by past immodesties, some of her most distinguished servants, scholars and saints have brought their considerable powers of ingenuity to bear. Pope John XXIII, for instance, simply explained: 'I am not infallible; I *am* infallible only when I speak *ex cathedra*; but I shall never speak *ex cathedra*.'[2] And he never did. Pope John was, I believe, giving expression to the insight shared by Charles Davis,[3] himself formerly a Roman Catholic priest. He said that lust is to love what certainty is to religion. Those who lust after certainty in religion know nothing of the love of searching faith. This apart, the claim of infallibility is both superfluous and self-defeating, for if the purpose of the church is to mediate the reality of God to the believer the infallibility of her teaching will be self-authenticating only to the degree that the believer knows through experience the reality of God. If such certitude is outside the believer's experience no

32

amount of insisting that the church's teaching is infallible will sound convincing or evoke the response of unquestioning obedience.

Another side of the church's pit of infallibility was shown by Professor Eduard Schillebeeckx during a visit to Birmingham University. He said that people who wanted to change the wording of the church's dogma hadn't 'a hope in hell'. I think they were his words, but if I have misquoted him I have given the exact meaning he clearly wished to convey. He went on to suggest that though the wording of dogma should be left well alone, believers should be allowed to make their own private interpretations. Well, that is another way of dealing with discredited infallible teaching. It rather reminds me of the story told by Hans Küng in his delightful book *Truthfulness: The future of the church*.[4] During the second Vatican Council he asked his friend, the American theologian John Courtney Murray, what was to be thought of a certain American archbishop. The reply came: 'He is an absolutely honest man. He would never lie except for the good of the church.'

Hans Küng himself, rejecting uncompromisingly and with detailed scholarship the Roman Catholic Church's traditional claims to infallibility, nevertheless makes it clear why and how he still believes in the infallibility of the church.

If the Church ceases to be in the truth, it ceases to be the Church. But the truth of the Church is not dependent on any *fixed* infallible propositions, but on her remaining in the truth throughout all propositions, including erroneous ones. Meanwhile, to emphasize the *truth* of the Church in relation to the *being* of the Church, let us for the sake of clarity talk, not of the indefectibility or perpetuity of the Church, but of its indefectibility or perpetuity in the truth. What is meant by this is that the Church remains in the truth, and that it is not affected by any errors in detail. This makes it plain that we hold fast to the fact of infallibility, though for the reasons given we prefer the terms 'indefectibility' or 'perpetuity'.[5]

His meaning is that the whole church, not just the Pope or the ecumenical council or the totality of bishops throughout the world, is the guarantee of infallibility; but infallibility only in this sense – that despite the church's mistakes, faulty judgments, deviations from truth through acts of deliberate disobedience and cowardly expediency, she always returns to God and again centres in him. The faith and devotion of the total church is like a gyroscope of infallibility which guarantees that whatever the vicissitudes of human frailty or wickedness the Body of Christ is somehow kept on course or sooner or later brought back on course.

Does all this mean, then, that questions of truth and false-hood are superfluous, if only because the answers either way are open to doubt and can never be resolved by methods acceptable to all parties? Clearly the difference between truth and falsehood is crucial, but perhaps not in the way some of us suppose. We now know that truth is not truth simply because it is declared to be so by an authoritative body, ecclesiastical or otherwise. The main criterion of truth is the degree to which it serves men, helps them to become whole, leads them to fulfilment, renews them to live responsibly. This, I believe, was the approach of Jesus of Nazareth. He knew that the only way to religious truth was by experiential knowledge; every man had to seek, discover and define the truth for himself. Such a way, though dangerous, was inescapable, unless the 'believer' was prepared to play safe within a straitjacket of dependent conformity. Jesus knew that some individuals wanted nothing more than to be told what to do and precisely how to do it. Sometimes they came to him with questions about the law,[6] how to divide an inheritance,[7] whether to pay taxes,[8] and like concerns. Almost invariably he turned the questions back in their direction, commenting but not answering. They were to decide for themselves. In the final analysis, as far as religious beliefs are concerned, we must do the same.

34

Now why is it, we must go on to ask, that religious beliefs appear to make so little difference in the lives of some people. We have already seen that it is not because they do not take their beliefs seriously or believe the wrong things, that is, things different from the beliefs of people for whom religion works to the end of wholeness. They *do* believe, with sincerity and what passes for orthodoxy, but still they feel empty of Christian virtue and give every impression of struggling to carry what should be supporting them. I wonder whether the explanation is somehow rooted in a possible difference between conscious belief and unconscious attitudes. Is it conceivable that people who believe one thing – believe with passion and proselytizing zeal – are unconsciously activated by something else? Our own elementary self-awareness surely provides a ready answer. In all manner of ways conscious belief and unconscious attitudes are out of harmony, a fact of experience usually perceived in retrospect.

The condition of unconscious rejection of conscious belief is beyond doubt. We believe one thing and do the opposite. Our sincerity is not at fault. No one is more bewildered or disappointed than ourselves. Yet clearly something other than renewed resolve to be consistent is required. As we seek to understand what it is, we must probe a little deeper.

It does seem as though *our* beliefs as distinct from the beliefs we accept only on someone else's authority, grow invariably out of experience. We find quite often that such experience is articulated convincingly for us in the language of historical Christianity; the creeds and other thought-forms or orthodoxy find a re-echo within us because they speak to and of our condition. This does not make them sacrosanct. It could be that in personal conversation we would express our convictions differently, but generally speaking the language of the church is meaningful in the crucial sense that it illuminates the inside of our personal experience. With others of us this is far from the case. Our experience appears to be in conflict with traditional religious language. We find it hard to articulate our convictions, the convictions that express our experiental knowledge of God or ultimate reality, but of one thing we are sure – so-called orthodoxy obscures rather than clarifies.

The trouble really starts when we feel obliged or are called upon to subscribe to religious teaching that does not make sense to us or harmonize with our deepest feelings, our intuitive affirmations of faith. We can't believe, yet we want to for honourable and dishonourable reasons, if they *are* dishonourable. For we want to believe because we want to belong. We want to belong because our friends and others whose approval we seek are in the church. We want to believe because we're afraid not to believe, afraid to face the rough and tumble of life without the security and comfort of our faith. The reasons why people want to believe are as varied as their faces, but in some cases there's little doubt that a major cleavage is caused by what they try to believe and what their experience of life unconsciously affirms as true.

There is something else, too. In numerous cases it seems that people's conscious beliefs are too weak to change their unconscious attitudes. What fashions them as persons is not primarily what they consciously believe, but the unconscious pressures which make up their personalities. It's true, and they know it's true, that faith can remove mountains and cast out devils, but they apparently lack the faith and do not know how to get it. The situation is made worse when they try to make their experience of life harmonize with the religious beliefs to which they want to subscribe for reasons other than the ones of which they are aware.

Bearing all this in mind, it seems to me that we have to come to terms with the insistence of Jesus of Nazareth that rules were made for men, not men for rules. Likewise doctrines were made for men, not men for doctrines. The temptation is to make the opposite approach with the result that life is tested against theology *before* theology is interpreted and perhaps re-written by life. I can only repeat that it is what we discover and prove for ourselves that represents the truth for us. Other people, articulating their understanding of truth in ways different from ours, might accuse us of heresy or worse and assert that we are adrift from God. They could be right. But the criterion will not be their judgment. It will be the extent to which we are becoming human, the quality of our personal relationships, whether or not we are easier to live with, our identity as real persons. If these factors are kept firmly in mind, I believe that we shall all be moving in the same direction and giving expression to the same spiritual realities.

NOTES

1. William Temple, *Nature, Man and God*, Macmillan 1934, p.317.
2. Quoted by Hans Küng in *Infallible?*, Collins 1971, p.71.
3. During a talk given on Radio 3 on Friday 18 February 1972.
4. Hans Küng, *Truthfulness: The future of the church*, Sheed & Ward 1968, p.99.
5. Küng, *Infallible?*, p.150.
6. Matt. 18.1–6; 19.3–9; Luke 20.27–38.
7. Luke 12.13–15.
8. Matt. 22.15–22.

The Touchstone of Truth

As far as the world within ourselves is concerned, we all recognize that when we state the truth in words we state less than the truth. I might, for instance, describe a sunset to a man born blind, but in the very telling – though what I say is factual – I know that my words are communicating much less than the whole truth about the sunset. The same applies to experiences of joy, awe, or sorrow; and is nowhere more true than in the world of religion, the world in which men experience the mystery of transcendence. One reason is that the quintessence of the experience is non-rational; it does not, as we have seen, supersede reason, it transcends it, points to another dimension of reality altogether. Hence the problem of articulation, for how can this sort of truth be trapped in words or be adequately communicated by definitions called dogmas or doctrines? Undoubtedly dogmas and doctrines have their place in aiding man's spiritual explorations; they are essential stages on the way to fuller understanding, but by their very nature they can never be more than resting places. If they are not provisional, which makes them none the less trustworthy, they are breeding grounds of bigotry, intolerance, and other forms of spiritual pride.

Probably more than anyone else, seminal thinkers in the realm of spiritual values face this problem of sharing their insights. Jesus of Nazareth was no exception. Men were enriched but also enslaved by their culture and religious traditions, enslaved to the extent of listening to him and hearing little or nothing. His words were distorted, wrongly interpreted in a fundamental sense, so that when he referred to God he meant one thing, but the Pharisees and like-minded religionists understood him to mean something quite different. His disciples, too, at times were equally clueless. To the end of his earthly life they made unintentional mockery of his efforts to initiate them into his greater understanding and experience of God. Even Jesus himself was sometimes staggered by their blindness and apparent inability to learn. The pathos of his words to Philip, 'Have I been all this time with you, and you still do not know me?',[1] indicates something of his disappointment and perhaps incredulity. Yet he was tenacious in trying to inform and enlighten: the kingdom of God is like this (and he described a woman baking bread)[2] or the kingdom of God is like that (and he talked about a man sowing seed).[3] Because words are so finite and convey at best only aspects of truth, he frequently appeared to contradict himself. On one occasion he said that 'he who is not with me is against me'[4] but on another 'he who is not against me is with me'.[5] He told his disciples to 'take no thought for tomorrow',[6] but also (in a parable) commended a double-dealer in business for having the ingenuity to make provision for his old age.[7] These apparent contradictions are of course complementary facets of truth, but they at least illustrate the difficulties facing the seminal thinker as he seeks to propagate his message. If he is fortunate his immediate disciples perceive the essential truth of his words and, following their master's death, if not before, seek in turn to teach his message or more particularly to share the new experience of their own discipleship. The trouble is that their words too are open to misunderstanding and like their master they too die, leaving their disciples or converts to propagate the supposed original teaching.

Once this teaching is written down and is evolved into a system of theology, still greater confusion occurs with the assumption that believing the creeds or some comparable statement of belief is identical to possessing the authentic experience of which the articles of faith attempt to speak. But they are never more than approximations or pointers in the direction of the reality. In consequence there is no guarantee that the most orthodox believer, simply because he is an orthodox believer, enjoys the richness of the experience with which the original teacher was concerned. This being so, we are inescapably confronted by the question: what is the nature of religious experience? More to the point, we have to ask how we know that a religious experience is authentic and not merely emotionalism or the result of a frantic search for comfort and protection. Indeed, is it possible ever to be *sure* that we are in touch with God, however conceptualized, and not just a projection made in our own image?

The complexity of this question was illustrated for me when I visited the convent of an Anglican contemplative order. The prioress received me and soon we were deeply embroiled in lively conversation. It was apparent that she was familiar with death-of-God theology and less extreme expressions of similar thinking. She treated it seriously with a tolerance that was not even tinged with self-conscious humility. There was no wish to avoid probing questions, to take refuge behind traditional dogmas, or to find easy answers by turning a blind eye to areas of theological ferment and controversy. Her own understanding of God was clearly anchored in the traditional teaching of the church, but she was open to the possibility that he was revealing himself to secular man in other equally valid ways. But only the possibility. Though agreeing that God is not restricted to our definitions or trapped within the current orthodoxies of the church this gracious woman was quietly persistent that anything short of conscious Christ-centred faith was less than ideal. This was corroborated by five senior sisters, nuns of long experience, with whom I was also permitted to talk unhurriedly. Like the prioress they testified that Jesus of Nazareth was indispensable to their own understanding of God, but – also like her – agreed that other individuals might well encounter him in seemingly non-religious ways and conceptualize that encounter accordingly. They spoke with the authority of personal experience, and their certitude *was* authoritative. It silenced all argument and made clear beyond doubt that their faith in God was the most real thing in their lives. Nevertheless they readily admitted that their assurance was no guarantee that they were in fact in touch with God. As the prioress said to me: 'We could be self-deluded, in which case our whole lives are futile and a waste.'

Her conviction that she was not self-deluded expressed itself, of course, in her continued presence at the convent, but we do well, I think, to bear her words in mind as we wrestle with the nature of authentic religious experience. It is not without significance that Alastair Kee, a minister of the Church of Scotland, and a university lecturer in theology, claims in his book *The Way of Transcendence*[8] that even Jesus of Nazareth was deluded about his experience of God. Dr Kee argues that just as Jesus was mistaken about the imminence of the coming of the kingdom of God so he was, being a man of his times, mistaken about God himself. For God, insists Dr Kee, does not exist. Furthermore the very idea of God is both increasingly unintelligible and unacceptable to western man. But this does not mean, the argument continues, that western man is no longer capable of religious experience. A Christian, says Dr Kee, is one who commits himself in faith with ultimate concern to the way of transcendence as represented by Jesus of Nazareth; and this commitment without reference to God is evidence that man is capable of self-transcendence at least in the sense that he is able and willing to commit himself to values that transcend his own immediate self-interest. To such matters we shall return.

The only point I want to make from Alastair Kee's book is that if a Christian minister, a man of Christ-centred faith, claims that Jesus himself was mistaken about his own experience of ultimate reality the question for all of us is surely related to the means, if any, of ascertaining what constitutes an authentic experience of transcendence. How can we be sure that we are not being led astray by pious ignorance, sincere misapprehension, religion without reality, and a way of thinking about God that is more the reflection of denominational taboos and touchy Puritanism than the result of an encounter with the God and Father of Jesus Christ?

The 'conversion' of Mary Slessor focuses the problem in extreme form. She was the member of a Sunday-school class whose zealous teacher was a dour Scot, an oldish woman who conceived it to be her duty to ensure that her teenage pupils 'gave their hearts to Jesus'. Her urgency to this end was motivated by her implicit belief in judgment and hell fire. Believing that 'the fulness of time had come' in her concern for the girls' spiritual welfare, she invited them to her little home for Bible study. Before they arrived she made up the fire; and immediately they arrived she put on another log and gave the already fiercely burning ones a poke. Sparks flew up the chimney, whereupon she told the girls that if they were not converted they would go to hell, into the fiery flames of eternal punishment. Mary was converted! It could be argued that, despite the threatening and coercive approach of the desperately sincere evangelist, God used the occasion to bring Mary to himself; and that this is proved by her subsequent life of missionary service. I would not wish to dispute such a contention. But honesty compels me to say that I have met people subjected to that kind of evangelical approach who have never recovered from it; they are still alienated from the church and have a twisted concept of the Christian faith. However, was Mary Slessor's conversion in such circumstances an authentic experience of God? Was she really apprehended by love which never manipulates its object or adopts methods inconsistent with its own nature to achieve its purposes?

Looking at this question of religious experience from another standpoint, I remember an old man who was, as we say, one of 'nature's gentlemen'. When he lost his wife he was utterly confounded, forlorn and lost. He withdrew into his own strictly-guarded world, rarely leaving the house and admitting no visitors. Finally my wife managed to see him and learned that he was having visions and hearing voices. They were real enough, and he certainly believed that they were 'not of this world'. There were occasions when he saw the devil dancing tauntingly at the end of the bed; some of the visions *were* devilish, and the old man, his conscience made perhaps over-sensitive by years of devout introspection, interpreted them as God's punishment.

We called in the doctor who quickly diagnosed malnutrition and arranged for the demented patient to be admitted to hospital. After a few good meals the visions and voices ceased. But the old man remained convinced that they were real in the sense that God had sent them. Nothing could persuade him otherwise. Yet surely we were right to conclude that the visions and voices were symptoms of malnutrition and nothing more. The old man's neglect of food caused the metabolism of his body to change to such a degree that he suffered hallucinations.

Something of the same sort happens when people take drugs, certainly if they take them persistently. The metabolism of the body changes, with the result that they too have visions and other hallucinatory experiences. This is sometimes called 'chemical' spirituality. Under the influence of drugs people *do* see and hear what otherwise is closed to them. Frequently they interpret these experiences in spiritual terms, talking about the transcendental or encounters with ultimate reality. They are convinced that the drugs introduce them to an extrasensory world and enable them to explore realities beyond the normal boundaries of time and space.

The history of Christian spirituality illustrates that spasmodically followers of Christ, believing themselves called to the ascetic life, have practised fasting on a punishing scale. They have lived on next to nothing, scourging their bodies for the supposed good of their souls. There seems little doubt that consequently some of them suffered from malnutrition, with the possibility – and it is no more than a possibility – that their visions and voices expressed more the unbalanced metabolism of their bodies than their fellowship with God. I mention this not to cast doubt on all spiritual experience, but simply to illustrate the complexity of knowing which experiences are authentic. How do we distinguish between what is trustworthy and what is pseudo? What are the infallible signs of authenticity in the realm of spiritual experience?

An Anglican priest, a friend of mine with long experience of working amongst the drop-outs and push-outs of society, describes religious experience as *any* experience that takes a man out of himself. He illustrates his meaning, or part of it, by referring to the football matches he occasionally watches on TV. When a goal is scored, he explains, the supporters of the team concerned go wild with excitement. They have a moment of ecstasy, are taken out of themselves, and transcend their immediate surroundings in a glimpse of 'glory'. It would be misguided, I believe, to dismiss such comments as irresponsible or ludicrously inadequate. The priest is not suggesting

44

that such a moment of ecstasy is a transcendental experience of any depth. He is, I think, feeling after the same sort of conclusion to which Peter L. Berger in his book *A Rumour of Angels* comes when he describes ordinary human experiences of a certain type as 'signals of transcendence'. This noted sociologist who first indicts radical theologians for selling out to the secularists – a comment which, I believe, only indicates that Professor Berger misunderstands what the theologians he has in mind are trying to say – goes on to suggest that joy, with its sometimes ecstatic moments of timelessness, and invulnerable hope point to reality beyond themselves. They are intimations of ultimate meaning. He also suggests that when a mother comforts her child in the night with such words as: 'Don't be afraid – everything is all right', she is giving an assurance that transcends the two individuals in their situation and is making a statement about reality in ultimate terms:

'*Everything* is in order, *everything* is all right' – this is the basic formula of maternal and parental reassurance. Not just this particular anxiety, not just this particular pain – but *everything* is all right. The formula can, without in any way violating it, be translated into a statement of cosmic scope – 'Have trust in being.' This is precisely what the formula intrinsically implies. And if we are to believe the child psychologists (which we have good reason to do in this instance), this is an experience that is absolutely essential to the process of becoming a human person. Put differently, at the very centre of the process of becoming fully human, at the core of *humanitas*, we find an experience of trust in the order of reality. Is this experience an illusion? Is the individual who represents it a liar?[10]

It is obvious that Professor Berger asks the two questions by way of underlining his conviction – his faith – that the order of reality can be trusted. But why? The Christian has his answer through the revelation of God in Christ. Not so Professor Berger and the mother he has in mind. They order their lives on the intuitive assumption that the statement of assurance – '*everything* is all right' – given by the mother in a common situation reflects the nature of the cosmos itself. Indeed, the professor is convinced, as we noticed, that the mother's reaction to her child's fear is a 'signal of transcendence', a confession of faith by a person who possibly never thinks of God in traditional terms.

Probably the many-sided nature of religious experience or the drive to transcendence is nowhere better illustrated these days than in the different ways people pray, even within the Christian tradition. This is not surprising, for it reflects, by the very nature of the case, the confusion surrounding the doctrine of God. When traditional teaching for whatever reason proves to be unsatisfactory, it is inevitable that the area in which the rejection of the old and the search for something new will be most apparent will be in the prayer life of the church and the private devotions of individual believers. We are able, all of us, to understand a little better what we believe about God by examining our concept and practice of prayer, for it is *there,* in the why and the how of our praying, that we discover both the nature of our faith in God and what we believe about him. Three real-life illustrations will indicate what I mean. The first is an expression of what some people might call secular prayer, and is given by W. H. Auden in his book *A Certain World*:

> To pray is to pay attention to something or someone other than oneself. Whenever a man so concentrates his attention – on a landscape, a poem, a geometrical problem, an idol, or the true God – that he completely forgets his own ego and desires, he is praying. Choice of attention – to pay attention to *this* and ignore *that* – is to the inner life what choice of action is to the outer. In both cases, a man is responsible for his choice and must accept the consequences, whatever they may be. The primary task of the schoolmaster is to teach children, in a secular context, the technique of prayer.[11]

46

It could be argued that such a concept of prayer is less than Christian, in so far as it does not consciously focus attention upon the God and Father of our Lord Jesus Christ or necessarily demand belief in him. But such an assessment would too easily provide an answer to a complex matter and possibly lose sight of a 'technique' of prayer which fundamentally is in harmony with the essential emphases of the New Testament.

The second illustration comes from Monica Furlong in her book *Travelling In*, and helps us to see the scope of prayer in terms of how each individual must of necessity discover the most suitable method for himself. She writes:

> What humiliates, looking back at one's attempts at prayer, is the pretentiousness of it all. The elaborate categories which were explained to me when I became a Christian – categories of praise and thanksgiving, of meditation and intercession. One dutifully tried to think oneself into gratitude and penitence and all the rest. I have never quite thrown off the sense of gloom and failure which hung over the whole attempt for me – I felt like a mongol trying to learn Greek. Part of the misery had to do with the talk of relationship with God. I hoped for something not unlike a daily telephone conversation with God, and was hurt that He seemed undisposed to chat. One's pride and pretentiousness does not much like the alternative, however, which is the scaling down of prayer to something utterly simple, and non-active. Sitting. Trying to inhabit oneself, and to set oneself within the landscape. When one achieves it praise is the natural response.[12]

There are doubtless many Christians whose experience of prayer in more traditional ways, wholly satisfactory for them, tempts them to question, if not deny, the validity of Monica Furlong's prayer life. After all, her 'technique', though doubtless evolved through trial and error, disillusionment, and not a little suffering, hardly appears to be in keeping with customary ideas of Christian prayer. Yet Monica Furlong and

47

people like her are undisturbed simply because their method of prayer is real and makes prayer real for them.

There was a time when manuals of devotion, each distinct in its approach to spirituality, were unanimous in their general suppositions about the one to whom prayer was to be made and the manner in which it was made. Such instruction is no longer acceptable or even intelligible to many people. They find that prayer as normally understood is meaningless and at best a source of little more than deadening artificiality.

This was powerfully brought home to me by a woman whose life was made insufferable by her attempts to pray within the traditional teaching of her church. She tells her own story, and I quote at length, not only because the document has exceptional intrinsic interest, but also because the question it finally poses is being variously heard on a growing scale. 'In many thousands of homes where the parents are devout', she says, 'young children begin and end each day kneeling in prayer at bedside or knee. I have no memory of thinking about it at all in any way different from other habits of teeth cleaning, washing or three meals a day. After breakfast family prayers were something to be hurried to be in time for school and assembly prayers – somehow they merged. Going to boarding school at ten years of age provided two years of feelings of superiority. After all, the four or five of us in my dormitory who knelt night and morning were much "holier than" the rest. So priggishness was a main characteristic of teen years. Other abstentions of mine helped, engendered by the Puritan background, but the seeds were sown before I thought at all.

'One way I differ from some was in a trait in my anxious mother. She did not much like the girl who came home from boarding school. My habit of blushing when blamed for misdemeanours convinced her of my guilt. If the gate hinges were loosened by my brother or sister swinging on them I was still the one who blushed. Whether I was guilty or not she could not bear to speak directly to me for days or a week until – crushed by the "atmosphere" – I was willing to comply and in the way which may well be the key. She insisted that I pray, at her bedside as she lay there, asking for forgiveness for the deceit, lie or whatever and also for her week of suffering!

'The priggishness remained; I was proud that I had read the Bible through twice by the time I was fifteen, proud that I never told a lie, proud that I prayed now virtuously. Then came the months when, allocated half an hour a day for private prayer, I could not admit that I found it difficult. Then marriage and a small family of my own, which unexpectedly meant the beginning of despair. Small children interrupt prayer. Tired, weary, and condemned as I began to miss a day here and there and then increasingly, I began to write a prayer diary. If I had my "prayer time" it was full of guilt for the lack of desire, for the days I had missed. If I did not pray the days were dark indeed. It is hard to convey sixteen years of this increasingly frequent depression. Towards the end, the darkness never lifted at all, but the diaries went on, each year's more empty.

'For me it was true that when you reach rock bottom then God must take over. One day as I was preparing to go to a Woman's World Day of Prayer meeting I was told by someone who had suffered much at the hands of my despair, that I was not *fit* to go. Wandering the streets, something I had read came to me. "God made you, not the good, pure, holy person you admire, but the failing, miserable, depressed person you are. He made your environment and your forebears. He's in your present situation". Somehow I was bold enough to shift that terrible overwhelming guilt I'd carried so long on to God's shoulders. I began life again, but I could not pray. In fact I dared not. For me to be a Christian was suddenly not what I did, but what I really wanted, the direction of my life. The true desires were me – not the conventional ones. There

49

could be no prayer, no communion with God, no intercession, no confession, no praise and gratitude in words; but the quality of life improved.

'For eight years now I have tried to find out what I truly want and level that up to my concept of truth. Time given in worship for prayer is spent in that way. Throughout those dark years I tried reading the prayers of others, attended a week-end Quaker school of prayer, everything anyone suggested (although I never told anyone my difficulties, I was too guilty).

'The freedom only came in abandoning prayer altogether. Can one never pray and be a Christian? Can this absolute necessity be discarded and God never spoken to, and can I still be accepted by the Church?'

Dare we conclude that this woman knows nothing or little of authentic religious experience? In our search for an answer, or at least the essential pointers in that direction, we are, of course, bound to ponder the New Testament; and when we do so the issue is clear-cut. In the four gospels and the epistles alike, the only criterion of judgment as far as authentic religious experience is concerned is the quality of life it generates. Encounter with God, fellowship with the source of all being, issues in spiritual and moral vitality. 'By their fruits you shall know them,' said Jesus of Nazareth.[13] He reiterated the emphasis time and again. 'Not everyone that *says*, Lord, Lord, but he that *does* the will of my Father.'[14] The 'blessed', he taught, are those who know that they are poor, who are sorrowful, have a gentle spirit, hunger and thirst to see right prevail, show mercy, whose hearts are pure, who are peacemakers, and suffer persecution for the cause of right.[15] The quality of life, which he exemplified and sought to share, is finally as indefinable as it is easy to recognize. Jesus of Nazareth underlined it explicitly in such parables as the Good Samaritan[16] and the Sheep and the Goats,[17] but it was implicit in everything he did and said.

The apostle Paul wrote about this same quality of life in terms of the 'harvest of the Spirit' – love, joy, peace, long suffering, gentleness, patience, goodness – insisting that such functional qualities were generated by the indwelling Holy Spirit.[18] The problem is that these noble words – this catalogue of virtues – do not get us far in our understanding of the good life. They represent something of crucial importance, we realize, but exactly what it is we are not able to say in anything like the precise terms we would wish. Simone Weil, French philosopher and mystic, was referring to it, I believe, when she wrote:

> Workers need poetry more than bread. They need that their lives should be a poem. They need some light from eternity. Religion alone can be the source of such poetry. It is not religion but revolution which is the opium of the people.[19]

By 'religion' she meant something far more than institutional religion, something with which she herself never was able to come to terms in her unhappily shortened life (she died in England from malnutrition during the Second World War through so austerely identifying herself with life in occupied France). I believe that she was referring to that mystical element which transforms people into real persons, and speaks of inward richness rather than outward riches.

Men are aware as never before, it seems to me, that life is more than material prosperity, the possession of *things* in greater abundance. This is discernible not least in the work of social service agencies, which are increasingly concerned to provide not only physical necessities but also the opportunity for people to share another dimension of human experience. In their commendable crusading for social justice, younger people notably are inclined to overlook this. They imagine that to lend a helping hand at a point of real need is identical to meeting more fundamental need which usually is less obvious and more complex. To dig an old person's garden, for instance, is helpful; to visit the sick, run errands, decorate shabby homes, and otherwise engage in community service is equally praiseworthy. But two things should not be ignored: the spirit in which such service is given can leave the individuals supposedly benefited feeling impoverished and less sure of themselves as persons of intrinsic value; and also that such service can become so obsessed with symptoms of need that root causes are either not recognized or accepted as regrettable parts of the *status quo*.

Man does not *live* by bread alone. He needs it and sometimes is compelled to depend upon more favourably placed people to provide it, but essentially he wants to share the good life as distinct from merely the good things of life; and this is possible only to the extent that he is a whole person in body, mind and soul. The word *soul* is important, though again a precise definition is impossible. It speaks of that mystical or mysterious element within man that makes him human. Without it, life not only loses its tone and dignity, but becomes a mockery of its own inherent potentiality.

Social workers of the Welfare State and their counterparts in voluntary service agencies know that it is comparatively easy to keep the boy on probation within the law, to help the unmarried mother to cope, to support the alcoholic in his attempt to stay dry, to get the old couple re-housed, but to enable such people really to *live*, to come alive as whole persons, is another matter altogether. The problem is that despite appearances to the contrary, they remain frightened, anxious, suspicious, self-rejecting, and secretly despairing.

They need *soul*, which is not to be confused with churchgoing, Bible reading, prayer and other usual associations of organized religion. These disciplines help some people, and doubtless they could help far more, but in themselves they do not inevitably produce the depth or richness of life with which we are concerned. Having a soul or that quality of life of which it speaks is more a question of loving and being loved, of feeling a sense of personal significance, of being free to grow as both a personality and a responsible member of society, of developing meaningful relationships and being treated always as an end, never a means.

Now this quality of life is found beyond doubt both inside and outside the church. It is found inside, let there be no mistake about that, but equally emphatically it is found outside. I sometimes get the impression that Christians are reluctant to admit that people outside the institutional church are anything but wicked sinners in need of God's forgiveness. They appear to want 'outsiders' to be notoriously sinful if only because this makes self-evident the truth of the claim that people are incapable of real virtue until their sins have been forgiven and they have been reconciled to God – strictly in ecclesiastical terms. However, if quality of life is, as Jesus said, the final touchstone of judgment, it is indisputable that there are individuals outside the institutional church but inside the kingdom of God.

Paul Tilich talks about the 'latent' church – that great body of people outside the institution who nevertheless live the Christian life. Karl Rahner, the Roman Catholic theologian, writes about the 'anonymous Christian' – the man who likewise lives in the spirit of Christ without conscious reference to Jesus of Nazareth. Commenting on this aspect of Karl Rahner's teaching, Anita Roper,[21] a German lay theologian, illustrates this point by dividing people into four distinct categories. There are Christians who live the Christian life; there are Chrisians who do not live the Christian life; there are non-Christians, meaning in this context simply non-institutional church members, who live the Christian life; and there are non-Christians who do not live the Christian life. She gets to the heart of Rahner's teaching by asking who is to decide into which category anyone is to be placed.

The same question is posed in a different way by Dorothee Sölle, another German lay theologian whose book *Christ the Representative*[22] revealed both her devoutness and penetrating perception. In a piece evocatively entitled 'Atheistic Belief in God'[23] she recalled a conversation she was informed about by a friend. He was a West German Christian who talked with some East German Marxists about the two ideologies or faiths. They made little headway. The Marxists understandably supposed that the encounter was one of theism and atheism, between 'acceptance of a traditionally constituted heavenly or personal "Other" and rejection of any such conception'. Consequently there was initially no real dialogue or openness to the opposite point of view.

'Only very gradually', wrote Dorothee Sölle, 'did my friend succeed in persuading the Marxists that the fronts of thinking today run across boundaries of political and ideological blocks. After some time, the Marxists admitted to my friend that he evidently was a real atheist like them because he, like them, did not need a conception of God to explain the world, to assure himself of a life after death, or to be able to feel happier here on earth. So then, the real conflict in the discussion sprang from much more profane and concrete things – in fact largely from the question, whether an individual in society can claim a right to his education, or whether he is entitled to a free choice of career and status. It is in such questions that the real argument between the Christian and Marxists materialized; *only when it was no longer concerned with theism or atheism but with people did the discussion recover its passionate seriousness*' (my italics).

Despite fundamental differences of belief, the individuals who shared that conversation discovered that to all intents and purposes they were one in their aims and hopes for society.

They cared about people, wanted to work for the same values, and generally to foster peace, justice, and freedom. Theoretically they were miles apart in their thinking to the point of deadlock, but in terms of common purpose for the welfare of the whole community they apparently did or sought to do the same things. Their strong ideological differences appeared not to matter. Dorothee Sölle commented: 'Such dialogues are now taking place in many parts of the world; the first remarkable thing is the breaking down of former differences of opinion which have, in the past, crystallized around the conception of God. My Christian friend by no means stands alone with his radical thought; it is an integral part of his approach to dialogue that he forces everyone who uses the word "God", whether Christian or non-Christian, to say exactly what he means by it – "exactly", not in terms of a philosophical definition, but in concrete, world terms. Whoever says "God" must be able to show what the word asserts about people in their relationships, and what is meant to be expressed by it in the partnership context. Everything else, all other untranslated talking about God in theistic terms is prohibited in such discussion.' Dorothee Sölle is convinced that the word 'God' is symbolic for many people of a 'way of life', a way which aspires after, and seeks to facilitate, a life of individual and corporate richness and fulfilment. It represents depth and diversity; its primary concern is quality.

With this in mind, I believe that any experience that makes a man more human and thereby both directly and indirectly contributes to the humanizing of society is a religious experience. *Any* experience! The only requirement is that it leaves the one concerned that much more sensitized to the values to which Jesus of Nazareth gave priority; values which people are stumbling over and discovering for themselves in all manner of situations and so-called secular experiences. The late Archbishop William Temple was of the opinion that religious experience is the whole experience of a religious person. But exactly who is a religious person? Essentially he is, I believe, simply a man in whose life there is that distinctive quality we have called soul or spirit; or at least a man whose face is turned in that direction. *That*, and that alone, appears to be the mind of Christ.

Let it be clearly understood that this quality of life is not synonymous with fastidious morality, the fierce fulfilment of the letter of the moral law. Jesus of Nazareth made the point to people whose religion was centred in an observance of touchy morality that 'traitors and prostitutes go into the kingdom of God before you'.[24] He was not condoning the behaviour of traitors and prostitutes, but he was stressing that the spirit for which he was looking was sometimes found in the most surprising people and places; and that it was infinitely more than cold morality. There are people, as we all know, on whose moral standards one cannot place a finger; they are scrupulously careful not to offend or deviate from the highest way of personal righteousness. Yet they give the impression of being more lawful than loving, and rarely overcome the temptation to put outward appearances before inward attitudes. And is that not the greater sin – devoutly to trivialize what is great and prostitute what is holy? Such a question must be asked, I think, if we are to understand with deeper penetration the quality of life which Jesus of Nazareth exemplified and sought to share.

Secular man is concerned to discover what is the good life, the just society, the meaning of being human and knowing freedom from fear in every otherwise crippling situation. He wants to know more about 'coming alive', of experiencing what Jesus called life in all its fulness. His ambition is to live before he dies. He is not impressed by our insistence that faith in Christ as we teach it is the key. Undoubtedly it is for some people, but secular man looks at the church and is not convinced that we represent the quality of life he seeks and certainly wants in his best moments. It could be that he is unjust in his criticisms and misunderstands the life of the people of God. It could be! But for whatever reason he is certain that – from what he has seen and heard of our faith and its practice – we have nothing helpful to contribute to his understanding of life.

Without surrendering our beliefs or compromising our commitment to the institution of the church, is it possible to look at religion and religious experience from another standpoint altogether, one immediately relevant to the multitudes of people outside the influence of the church? I believe it is.

NOTES

1. John 14.9.
2. Matt. 13.33.
3. Matt. 13.4–9.
4. Matt. 12.30.
5. Luke 9.50.
6. Matt. 6.34.
7. Luke 16.8.
8. Alastair Kee, *The Way of Transcendence*, Penguin Books 1971, pp.206–14.
9. Peter L. Berger, *A Rumour of Angels,* Allen Lane the Penguin Press 1970, p.20.
10. Ibid., pp.72–3.
11. W. H. Auden, *A Certain World*, Faber & Faber 1971, p.306.
12. Monica Furlong, *Travelling In*, Hodder & Stoughton 1971, p.52.
13. Matt. 7.20.
14. Matt. 7.21.
15. Matt. 5.3–12.
16. Luke 10.30–37.
17. Matt. 25.31–46.
18. Gal. 5.22–3.

19. Simone Weil, *Gravity and Grace*, Routledge & Kegan Paul 1963, p.159.

20. Paul Tillich, *On the Boundary*, Collins 1967, p.67.

21. Anita Röper, *The Anonymous Christian*, Sheed & Ward, NY 1966.

22. Dorothee Sölle, *Christ the Representative*, SCM Press 1967.

23. Dorothee Sölle, *Atheistisch an Gott glauben*, Walter-Verlag, Olten. The book has not been translated into English.

24. Matt. 21.31.

4

Religious Experience without Belief in God

When the brilliant Marghanita Laski, a self-confessed atheist, was taking part in a radio discussion about the New English Bible, she expressed her preference for the Authorized Version. The reason, she explained, was that the Authorized Version facilitated religious experience; its beauty of language, suggestive of the mystical and the mysterious, of the dimension to life called spiritual, was more conducive to experiences of transcendence than the pedestrian, though doubtless clearer, language of the New English Bible. Miss Laski concluded her remarks with the exclamation: 'We all need religious experience!'

There are people who rather resent such atheistic aspirations. They feel that the Marghanita Laskis of this world should not try to have their cake and eat it; that if they do not believe in God they have no right to talk about religious experience, for this, it is confidently assumed, is clearly contingent upon personal belief or faith in the existence of God. There is no doubt, however, that atheists and the more numerous humanists who call themselves agnostics, disagree. Ronald Hepburn, for instance, writing a critique of humanist theology in *Objections to Humanism*, commented:

> There are certain types of religious experience, seen as the 'holy', some forms also of mystical experience that, for some

people at least, can continue to occur even in agnosticism. They seem in this sense to be 'autonomous', not belief-dependent, experiences. Even if they are not seen as yielding new knowledge of the world, insights into 'ultimate truth', they can still make a profound mark on a person's moral outlook. They can do so, not by imparting specific new information or specific rules of conduct but by nourishing a sense of wondering openness to new ways, new possibilities of life. They implant a disturbing restlessness, an intensified dissatisfacton with the mean, drab, or trivial.[1]

In conversation with all sorts of people I have heard this kind of emphasis made time and again. A typical comment was uttered by a woman in her early twenties who was as sure of God as she was certain that she did not believe in him after the manner of institutional religion: 'I don't know much about religion,' she said, 'I only know about people; that's what I look for as the ultimate meaning . . . I mean the ultimate thing for me is not to have to think about anything but just to *be*. It doesn't happen very often. There is always something to be conscious of, very few times when I'm not just conscious of anything but myself, and perhaps another person. Really it's just me because I feel real. I can't say that on such occasions I've thought about God, but it's the nearest I'll get to it because the more we talk about it the more I'm sure that God isn't separate, not a cut-off thing. He's part of it; I believe He's sort of in it.' The testimony was given hesitantly, the speaker groping for words, but there was no doubting her central point – that G–O–D, whatever that symbol means, is to be experienced, not talked about. Those who say don't know; those who know don't say. But though they don't say, or say adequately, despite their sometimes earnest attempts, they are characterized by their openness to life. The degree of openness varies from experience to experience, and from day to day, but the attitude of wonder is fundamental. Obviously it is not restricted to adherents of orthodox religion; people of belief and non-belief have it. All we can say is that without it belief is dead and with it non-belief is alive.

The spirit of wondering openness I have in mind has three distinctive elements. First of all its outlook is one of eager expectation, like hope on tiptoe. It greets every day as a new beginning, an adventure waiting to be unfolded. Without being frantic or smothered by excitability, it approaches life with the conviction that serendipity* – what C. S. Lewis called being 'surprised by joy' – is not exclusive to special occasions. It *expects* to be surprised by joy, and often is. Significantly most of these 'surprises' take place within routine activities. In other words they reflect more inner life than outward circumstances. People usually find what they seek! When life seems drab or uneventful this spirit of expectation is patient – waits with purpose, confident that every experience yields its riches to those open to receive them. When discouragement and depression descend, far from being stifled, the attitude of wonder reminds itself that *this too will pass*. And it does, facilitated by the assurance that it will.

The second element is receptivity, the capacity to receive. Few people have it. Most of us are better at accumulating than receiving. To accumulate is straightforward enough and requires little more than application. I want something so I work and save until I get it. This achieved, I move on to the next acquisition, possibly mystified that the last one, for all my struggling to possess it, brought far less pleasure than I expected. Receiving is a different matter altogether. It is a gift, yet one that I must earn. We sometimes say that a person is gifted, meaning that he is naturally talented in some outstanding way, but he still needs to earn his gift, practise self-denial in the interests of whatever it is he has the potential to

*'The faculty of making happy and unexpected discoveries by accident' (*Oxford English Dictionary*).

do well. If he doesn't earn his gift it goes away, possibly never to return. Now this capacity to receive operates similarly, but still it remains essentially a mystery. The most surprising people have it. Some are rich, others poor; some healthy, others chronically sick or handicapped; some escape trouble, others get more than their share. The one thing they have in common is their ability to receive which, they are quick to explain, they did not consciously learn at all. What is certain is that such people live in a spirit of wondering openness. Without despising tangible riches, they are first of all committed to things that money cannot buy. As John G. Mac-Kenzie once wrote in another connection, they seek on earth the things that can also be found in heaven; and whether you think of heaven as future bliss or the ideal NOW the point he was making is crystal clear. Beyond doubt *receiving* is a way of life. It is the natural consequence of inner orientation, of what it is we seek first. Without it the most privileged life is impoverished. With it the most deprived life is an exploration of astonished joy.

How to get it? I wish I knew, apart from saying that it comes or grows usually slowly as we drop our pre-judgments, learn that love is more reliable than law, that people are more important than principle, and allow our souls to be nourished by the gift of wonder. Sounds vague, I agree, but life, after all is primarily for living, not verbalizing.

Apart from expectation and receptivity, the spirit of wondering openness includes the element of creativity. To be creative is something of which we are all potentially capable. The fact that too many of us hardly ever begin to move in this direction is related, I believe, to the absence of serendipity. Paradoxically the marvels of modern technology have drained life of its wonder. Instead of prompting within us a spirit of speechless awe, the latest moon shot finds us looking for a bit of excitement and wondering how much longer the TV programmes are going to repeat themselves; we've seen it all before.

The creative person is by no means always outstandingly talented. Indeed, creativity has little to do with the ability to *do*. It is more directly related to the capacity to *be*. In other words, creative persons are authentic and real. They are free to live because they live to be free. The freedom that concerns them is not, needless to say, a polite synonym for licence; such supposed freedom is itself an enslavement and proves itself so by destroying or hindering creativity.

To be creative is responsibly to do your own thing. I insert the word *responsibly* with a measure of reluctance, not because I want to encourage people to do their own thing irresponsibly, but because many individuals are stifled by nothing more than their preoccupation with trying to be responsible. Their concept of the word is like a straitjacket or – to use another of C. S. Lewis's phrases – like a 'mental corset'. It narrows the mind and reduces the number of possibilities by turning responsibility into frightened or resented conformity. Creativity insists that a man be true to himself, not the self conditioned by other people's ideas and demands, but his own thinking and feeling. For he will live creatively only to the degree that he explores and adventures, following truth as he perceives it and having the courage to obey first his own integrity. The world is full of people who are pathetic caricatures of themselves through listening to prohibitions created by a society – family or wider community – obsessed with security and the orderliness of undisturbed sameness. The obsession is understandable enough, and doubtless represents voices to which every wise man will grant a hearing, but still finally *he* (not they) should decide, whatever the cost in terms of their disapproval and misunderstanding.

That there are dangers and subtle pitfalls in such a way of life goes without saying, but they are less lethal than the safer alternatives and, unlike them, all of them, they carry the promise of fulfilment as a distinct possibility. The great safeguard is, of course, that personal creativity is exercised always with sensitive regard for the freedom of other people also to be creative. To intrude upon them or otherwise to restrict their creativity is sure evidence of egocentricity or self-deceit, with the inescapable destructive repercussions always at hand.

These three elements within the attitude of wondering openness to the whole of life demand, to use Paul Tillich's inspired book title, the 'courage to be'.[2] Not the courage to do or not to do; that is sometimes fiercely demanding but still comparatively easy. The courage to *be* is a different proposition altogether and can be no one else's responsibility but my own. I might achieve success in countless fields, occupy a position of power and prestige, amass a fortune or at least possess enough to impress both the neighbours in our rising middle-class district and the undiscerning with my ability to get on and go up. Conversely I might fail at everything, be overdrawn at the bank, have no official influence, live in a one-up-and-one-down with the privy outside, and generally give the impression of inglorious mediocrity. But appearances in either case might well be deceptive. At any event, the reality belongs to the world within myself, for I am a human being or more correctly a human becoming. Ideally the process never stops; I grow in freedom and capacity to love, I learn my true identity and say *yes* to it without pride or apology, I experiment with life always against the touchstone of authenticity, the opposite of sham and lust for security. If I do not, whatever appearances to the contrary I manage to maintain, I exist in a torturous vacuum and remain shut tight to the gift of wonder. Increasingly my life becomes artificial, made up of the inconsequential jockeying for position with the trivial.

Now wonder, like every other expression of creativity, is both spontaneous and the result of self-discipline. It happens inexplicitly, but also needs to be facilitated. A man is possessed by wonder, sometimes unexpectedly, at other times as a result of going out to meet it. Without being able to manufacture it, he can place himself in its way; take time to nourish its spirit within the routine of obligation. But there is no guarantee that he will know the spirit of wonder simply by seeking it, at least seeking it according to somebody else's terms of reference. Inevitably people will tend to feel reverence for life in the face of common experiences, but not necessarily so. One man's wonder is another man's boredom, though the latter might not be prepared to admit it. He mistakes wonder for, say, aesthetic appreciation, which means that he possibly wanders round an art gallery trying desperately to be impressed by what somebody else tells him is beautiful. He does not look at the pictures so much as look at himself looking at the pictures. In the same way, he does not listen to the concert so much as listen to his own complimentary references to his good taste. He knows that he should be impressed in the presence of a beautiful sunset, and reacts accordingly, but his mind is secretly elsewhere. In other words, he uses even his potential for wonder as a status symbol, one representing riches he does not possess and camouflaging his lack of response beneath impressive appearances. He apparently does not realize that wonder is always related to honest openness; it by-passes the man who plays a part – plays fast and loose with his own or anybody else's feelings, thinks more of being true to conventions than to himself.

It is this attitude of honest openness that exposes a man to the constant possibility of wonder or reverence for life. According to personality and background, people receive the gifts of wonder in widely varied ways, but never do they receive it without honest openness. In itself this suggests that our capacity for wonder is proportionate to our inner security, our willingness to adventure and our sense of mystery or, as I prefer in this context, our sense of miracle. For the understanding of mystery does not always remove the element of miracle; sometimes it emphasizes it. My two sons were present when their wives gave birth to their babies. The experience was infinitely more than enlightening. It was awe-inspiring, a time of miracle. They each knew in general terms what to expect, but the event proved to be – incredible. Why? It certainly was not because they did not understand it. Indeed, the more they understood what was happening the greater was their reverence and wonder at the miracle of life.

It is this attitude or spirit to which I refer when I say that belief in God is not primarily a matter of words and their meaning but of living religiously. There are religious people – sincere and devout – who know far too little of what it means to live religiously. They practise religion as a compensation for their insecurity and unadventurous approach to the whole of life; fastidiously insist upon outward conformity as a substitute for inward vitality. They worship God with their lips but deny him with their incapacity for wonder. Of course there are also countless believers who know the glories of both worship and wonder; whose wonder, in fact, drives them to their knees in worship, and whose celebration of life finds expression in the sacraments of the church. But there are still multitudes representing a growing majority whose only religion is, I believe, the attitude to life I have suggested. They do not think of this attitude as religious and rarely share the observances of institutional religion, but they are, nevertheless, religious in the way that counts most. This is one reason why some people who do not believe in God, either by deliberate decision or by default, give the impression of being *alive* and of the company of Jesus of Nazareth. It stands to reason that they are truly followers of Christ. For they live in his spirit. Equally to the point, we feel in our very bones that they are discovering the truths of religion, no matter how they articulate them or ignore the conventions of ecclesiastical procedure. They *are* religiously orientated, despite their denial of religious belief. This orientation, as well as incorporating the elements of wondering openness, is characterized by a certain quality of life. How to define or describe it is difficult, apart from saying that Jesus of Nazareth exemplified it, but that, I realize, does not get us very far. It has nothing to do with perfectionism or the law of morality. Indeed, such ideas are its antithesis. This quality of life is finally too big for words, too elusive for hard and fast rules, too dynamic for systematized thinking. It is simply self-authenticating; immediately recognizable by its pulsating winsomeness. As I say, all sorts of people have it, inside and outside the institution of the church, with and without conscious faith in God. But wherever it is found the spirit of wonder is never far away.

Now almost inevitably this spirit of wonder makes a man want to worship or celebrate. If he is an orthodox believer he feels the impulse to bend the knee, bow the head, lift up the heart in adoration and thanksgiving. But if he is not, the same impulse possesses him. It expresses itself in totally different ways, but with the identical spirit of reverence, of awareness that one is in the presence of something *super*-human; more than human. John Wren-Lewis referred to such experiences when he wrote in *What Shall We Tell the Children?*:

I find a sense of awe both from the immediate contemplation of the elementary fact of creativity in myself and the others I see around me, but even more from an objective contemplation of the way the human species as a whole has never ceased to struggle for new levels of health, knowledge, aesthetic beauty and civilization, in spite of the immense conservative forces of fear, prejudice, stupidity, meanness, selfishness and hypocrisy. In fact I get a sense or a hunch of 'a power or presence which is somehow superior to man as we ordinarily know him', not so much from particular humanistic concerns like beauty or ecstasy or love or stillness, as from the very

67

basis of all humanistic concern, the power of imagination, the creativity of the human spirit itself.[3]

People who once described themselves as atheists or agnostics, sometimes not without evidence of intellectual pride, and who in consequence felt themselves obliged to take up a position of antagonism to institutional religion are now, I believe, not so sure. They still have no time for institutional religion, but the dimension of human experience the church represents is not so readily or cheaply dismissed. Increasingly it is being recognized that such factors are related to questions of man's fundamental make-up or to the one big question of what it means to be human. In this connection, the old-fashioned humanism – with its dogmatic assertions that organized religion was corrupt or corrupting and based upon a belief in God that was wholly subjective to each individual believer – is discredited, as much discredited as the institution it once attacked appears to be to probably the majority of people in western society. Likewise materialism is rejected as totally inadequate to meet the needs and aspirations of *whole* persons. For *whole* persons, as Marghanita Laski reminded us, whatever their beliefs, need religious experience. They need religious experience, but not, they are convinced, of the variety that belongs inseparably to traditional religious belief. At least, if it does, then *religious* experience will remain for ever beyond their credulity. It seems too fantastic or unattractive to be true.

The fact remains, however, that people are discovering or becoming aware of 'a power or presence which is somehow superior to man as we ordinarily know him'. Such awareness does not represent belief in God, certainly not as traditionally presented by the church, but it points, I think, to experiential knowledge which the possessors, baffled and awed, are keen to explore in search of possible meaning. Colin Wilson summed up this aspect of their feelings in his book *The Occult*: .

Whenever I am deeply moved by poetry or music or scenery, I realize I am living in a *meaning* universe that deserves better of me than the small-minded sloth in which I habitually live. And I suddenly realize the real deadliness of this lukewarm contentment that looks as harmless as ivy on a tree. It is systematically robbing me of life, embezzling my purpose and vitality. I must clearly focus on this immense meaning that surrounds me, and refuse to forget it; contemptuously reject all smaller meanings that try to make me focus on *them* instead.[4]

Colin Wilson and the people who think like him are not Christians by standards of orthodox belief. They give their allegiance to no particular ideology and are suspicious of dogmatism, most of all when shown as representing some sort of divine mandate. But they no longer brashly push aside questions of religion as irrelevant. On the contrary, they recognize as never before that transcendental concerns are not strictly the preserve of conventionally religious people. They concern all of us who are committed to being human; taking seriously every aspect of man's total nature. And when we do *that* we are immediately confronted by what Paul Tillich described as 'the road to depth', which inescapably led, he said, to encounter with God:

The name of this infinite and inexhaustible depth and ground of all being is *God*. That depth is what the word *God* means. And if that word has not much meaning for you, translate it, and speak of the depths of your life, of the source of your being, of your ultimate concerns, of what you take seriously without any reservation. Perhaps, in order to do so, you must forget everything traditional that you have learned about God, perhaps even that word itself. For if you know that God means depth, you know much about Him. You cannot then call yourself an atheist or an unbeliever. For you cannot think or say: 'Life has no depth! Life itself is shallow! Being itself is surface only.' If you could say this in complete seriousness, you would be an atheist; but otherwise you are not. He who knows about depth knows about God.[5]

But does he? Is it as simple – or as profound – as that? Beyond doubt many people know a lot about depth, those occasions when time seems to stand still, surface appearances are pierced, and meaning of some sort is positively intimated. It need hardly be said that for most people such meaning is not an initiation into the mysteries of God, neither is it related to the teaching of the church; indeed, it seems that these moments of depth are rarely interpreted as religious in any conventional sense at all. But their impact, fleeting or lasting, *is* related to the core of one's own life and perhaps to an awareness of something real that points to, or suggests, reality beyond itself. For the moment, however, I do not want to get bogged down trying to analyse these experiences of intense aliveness which rivet us to the spot, send shivers up and down the spine, induce silent wonderment and afford some insight into possible meaning. We do not so much comprehend the meaning as feel apprehended by the conviction that somehow there *is* meaning, and this in itself adds point to life and makes demands of us. *Yes, it makes demands.* We know it and want to respond. But it is more than demand, far more. There is what I can only call a *givenness* about such experiences: We know ourselves to be judged and yet accepted at the same time. On these occasions – which I confess are rare but memorable for me – I begin to understand how penitence is a sort of celebration; I feel shame and assurance, the healing pain of growing self-awareness, the, travail of wholeness. Martin Buber tried to pin-point the experience when he wrote:

> The reality is that we receive what we did not hitherto have, and receive it in such a way that we know it has been given to us. In the language of the Bible, 'Those who wait upon the Lord shall renew their strength.' In the language of Nietzsche, who in his account remains true to reality, 'We take and do not ask who it is that gives.'[6]

This is true for all manner of people, but again the more we wrestle to articulate the reality the more conscious we become of barely scratching the surface of meaning. I remember talking to a psychiatrist, a devoted Christian, about why he believed in God. 'Good question,' he replied; and was then silent for some minutes. The answer he attempted puzzled me more at the time than it does now. He explained that in connection with his work he occasionally found it necessary to read a lecture or an article he had written perhaps three or four years before, and as he read he thought to himself: 'I didn't write this; I couldn't have written this.' Far from wanting to suggest that his reaction indicated the brilliance of the writing, the psychiatrist was underlining his conviction that there was more *givenness* to his work than unaided achievement; that in retrospect he often found evidence that a greater wisdom than his own had been at work. Obviously this proves nothing, and as an isolated instance it has little significance, but related to the psychiatrist's total experience of life, which compelled him, he assured me, to use God-talk as alone adequate to describe what he knows, it surely represents a pointer we cannot ignore in our search for greater understanding.

There are individuals, of course, for whom such talk is neither necessary nor intelligible. Nevertheless, they too on occasion are aware of this *givenness* at the heart of their experience, a givenness which suggests Other, though precisely what that means they least of all are able to say; but the reality of the experience is beyond dispute and within it, it seems to me, are all the ingredients of what the Bible calls salvation. I make this suggestion because sometimes the purpose of the whole exercise resembles a kind of rescue bid, a reaching out that generates hope, the enemy of crippling despair.

The Christian at this point talks about *grace*, a word which speaks of loving initiative and unconditional acceptance in an ultimate sense, the sort of acceptance that affirms selfhood and the potential it represents. Non-Christians, believers in God or not, fellow-travellers on the road to depth who 'take and do not ask who it is that gives', use other terms, perhaps wholly secular, but this is not the main issue. What we want to know is whether the common experience of depth is rooted in the same reality. Is God or whatever being encountered by some other name? Harvey Cox, though not prepared to give an unequivocal *yes*, was in little doubt when he wrote *The Secular City*. 'The difference between men of biblical faith and serious non-theists', he said, 'is not that we do not encounter the same reality. The difference is that we give that reality a different *name*, and in naming it differently, we differ seriously in the way we respond.'[7] Of course, it cannot be *proved* that theists and serious non-theists experience the same reality. They appear to do, but beyond that we cannot go.

The same applies to all human experience, even that shared by people within a common religious faith. Two believers or more talk about their experience of the living Christ, but clearly it is quite impossible to know whether they are referring to an identical reality. Indeed, when the religious experience of, say, a Roman Catholic is compared with that of a Pentecostalist or primitive Methodist, the difficulty, despite their common language, of deciding whether they are in fact talking about precisely the same experience is self-evident. Undoubtedly they appear to be, but there can be no guarantee.

Assuming, however, that Harvey Cox is right in stating that theists and serious non-theists encounter the same reality, we have next to ask to what extent the naming of that reality changes the nature of the encounter. Put otherwise, we have to ask to what extent language *enables* and even changes experience. Supposing, for instance, that I have some sort of religious experience, one that I believe represents an encounter with God. In trying to make sense of it, to understand its meaning, I try to verbalize it and thereby run the risk, as we have seen, of obscuring rather than clarifying. The likelihood is that I finish up by analysing the experience almost out of existence. On the other hand, my attempt might well add weight to the experience, revealing aspects of its true nature to the degree of enriching and confirming it. In that case the explanation becomes a part of the experience itself and adds another dimension to it. Religious experiences or, as some people prefer, experiences of transcendence are not dependent upon religious belief no matter how defined. Theists and serious non-theists, we have supposed, encounter the *same* reality. But what they make of such encounters clearly affects the nature of their response and therefore, to a degree, the significance or impact of the encounters themselves.

There can be little doubt, then, that the naming of the reality determines the nature of the response. This is so in life generally. To be almost facetious, if a man had an experience of transcendence and attributed it to sentiment or indigestion his response would change the very nature of the experience itself. Far from being awed or inspired to wondering openness at new possibilities, he would be exasperated and confirmed in his scepticism, even cynicism. From this standpoint it clearly transpires that our understanding of religious experience affects the nature of the experience and determines its influence in our lives. If we forget or minimize this factor, as those romantics (not a term of abuse!) who insist that the experiential is exclusively the touchstone of reality and truth tend to do, we shall, I believe, be seriously misled and finally lose sight of our own complex make-up. For the experiential, which I certainly want to give its rightful place in our quest for understanding, is *experience plus interpretation,* inevitably; and the interpretation, consciously or unconsciously made, is bound to affect the nature of the experience itself. An essential element of any experience are the terms of reference by which the experience is judged. In other words, a man's concept of ultimate reality, how he sees himself against the landscape of life as a whole, is bound to affect at a profound level his very feelings and understanding of his experience. So Dietrich Bonhoeffer functioned in captivity and as he approached execution with a fearlessness bordering on gaiety because every aspect of his situation was coloured by his conviction about the ultimate. His creative response to the NOW was inspired by his presuppositions of faith, and those presuppositions largely determined the nature of his experience, what we are increasingly prone these days to call the experiential.

Sam Keen in his *Apology for Wonder* sums up what I am trying to say, from a slightly different standpoint:

> We are accustomed to thinking about physical and mental illness, but usually we do not apply the term pathology to philosophical world views and models of man. It is part of the anti-metaphysical bias of our age to assume that the way we view the ultimate context of human existence has nothing to do with sickness or health. Sickness results from germs, malfunctioning organs, disturbed human relationships, and possibly from political and social chaos, but not from mistaken or unbalanced philosophical ideas. My proposal is that pathology is indivisible; it has psychic, social and philosophical dimensions. Since man is that creature who constructs world views and models of himself, an unbalanced philosophy no less than disturbed personal relationships or inappropriate feelings is a symptom of illness.[8]

However, this is not to say that encounters with reality, unless interpreted in terms of so-called orthodox belief, lose their significance. The essential requirement is to find *meaning*, and it is in this area that convictions and opinions vary so considerably. People find meaning in their own way, influenced considerably by their background and culture, but not only so. For all sorts of reasons they interpret certain events – considered religious or not – as meaningful for them. In those events they find, perhaps *feel* is the better word, purpose, direction,

and what I can only call healing. And it is little use the orthodox believer dogmatizing that unless such experiences are
articulated in largely orthodox terms they are invalidated.

In the first place this is denied by all the evidence, and in the
second to *believe* statements of faith involves infinitely more
than merely offering mental assent. What surely needs to
happen is for people to be encouraged to respond in ways
meaningful to themselves, encouraged with tolerance and
openness to new insights. The churchman has no reason to
apologize or feel inferior because what was once considered
to be exclusive to the practice of religion appears to be available in different terms on a much wider front. Whatever
happens beyond the confines of the church, nothing alters the
fact that within her structures multitudes of people still find
sustenance for their souls and meaning in the area of experience we have been considering. The major difference today
in our understanding of religious experience is, I think, summed up by John Wren-Lewis: 'This insight – that transcendental concerns are in no way incompatible with a humanist
outlook – is equally important, I believe, for those who consider
themselves atheists or agnostics, for I suspect a great many such
people have rejected such concerns not for any really logical
reason but simply because they cannot accept the traditional
outlook with which such concern is identified.'[9]

Such a perceptive comment immediately suggests another
aspect of the response of theists and serious non-theists to
what Harvey Cox called 'the same reality'. It is, of course, the
question of worship, and to this theme we now turn.

NOTES

1. *Objections to Humanism,* ed. Blackham, Penguin Books
1965, p.50.
2. Paul Tillich, *The Courage to Be,* Collins Fontana Books
1962.

3. John Wren-Lewis, *What Shall We Tell the Children?*, Constable 1971, pp.122–3.

4. Colin Wilson, *The Occult*, Hodder & Stoughton 1971, p.177.

5. Paul Tillich, *The Shaking of the Foundations*, SCM Press 1949; Penguin Books 1962, pp.63–4.

6. Martin Buber, *I and Thou*, T. and T. Clark 1937, pp.109–10.

7. Harvey Cox, *The Secular City*, SCM Press 1965; Penguin Books 1968, p.270.

8. Sam Keen, *Apology for Wonder*, Harper & Row 1969, p.162.

9. Wren-Lewis, op. cit., p.111.

5

Worship of God is the Celebration of Man

A growing number of churchgoers are, I suspect, concerned that their congregational worship – and perhaps church life generally – seems unrelated to life. It appears to be an exercise that is external to real issues, an optional extra for people who enjoy that sort of thing, rather like an aesthetic capacity being indulged by those rare creatures who appreciate surrealist art; doubtless marvellous for them, but a bore for normal people. But surely worship belongs to the market place, pop festivals, the love of a man for a woman, laughing children, in fact to every area of human experience where life is celebrated with the result that people feel affirmed in their selfhood. After all, is that not one of the primary ways in which the authentic spirit of worship expresses itself?

There are individuals who talk about worship as being only of a certain order, who refer to a place of worship as though everything inside is more acceptable to God than anything outside, who restrict worship to what is holy, not what is whole. But long ago we were told that worship is more love than location, more relationship than ritual, more spirit than order. And certainly worship as reflected in the attitude of Jesus of Nazareth always feeds a man's self-respect – helps him to feel more of a man, more human, more of himself, a self that does not frighten him or make him ashamed. This is one reason, incidentally, why true worship is not always a happy experience. Thought of in terms of perpetual hymn singing and similar pleasures, it *is* for some people, and is assessed alone on that basis, but some celebrations in church and out open up unsuspected layers of self-understanding, and this can be a wretched experience. At such times the only consolation is the insight that such suffering is evidence of life, not the death it feels and suggests. For growing self-awareness is an essential element of progressive fulfilment.

Worship of God is not validated by words, genuflections, ceremonial observances, or other associations of religion. For some people, seemingly a shrinking minority, that is their way, and *clearly a valid way for them,* but it does not make sense to a greater number and is not related to their understanding of life. Such individuals, I imagine, will never learn to worship in traditional church terms. They certainly give no indication of moving in that direction. But they still want to celebrate, and indeed do, according to their own intuitive belief of what life is fundamentally all about. Whoever we are, churchgoer or not, the nature of our celebrations is, it seems to me, the nature of our faith. The two belong inseparably to each other and are mutually revealing.

Now I sometimes get the impression that church services, far from helping the worshipper to celebrate, encourage him to feel more worthless; good for nothing but to squirm under the condemnation of God's justice and be forgiven as a reward for suitable expressions of penitence. Not for one moment do I wish to suggest that within these traditional emphases – stated admittedly in extreme terms – there are not seeds of truth, but this is no reason to encourage excess in self-recrimination as a means of proving to God the sincerity of our desires to do better.

People with no knowledge of Christianity as represented sometimes by institutional religion, attending a place of

78

worship for the first time, might well get the impression that the worshippers were determined to underline their wickedness as a means of winning a greater measure of benefit from the one to whom their abject obeisance was being offered. I am not wishing to suggest that man is not sinful or that God's forgiveness is not needed; but surely most ordinary people, far from being arrogantly self-centred, are suffering from a sense of personal worthlessness. They feel of little use to anyone, lack confidence in themselves so that the slightest unusual demand finds them trying to dodge the issue and leaves them flustered and often floundering. Their habitual reaction to challenging situations is to feel inadequate, apologize for themselves by attitude if not word, and look for a concealed way of escape. There is at the centre of their lives a feeling of emptiness and fear, a crippling conviction that they are of no use and cannot cope. Some of them cover up this lack of belief in themselves by bluster and exaggerated self-importance. They impose and manipulate, shout and demand, boast and promise, push themselves forward and otherwise engage in forms of pompous (often unconscious) self-deceit. There are occasions, however, like those in the still hours of the night, when they catch a glimpse of themselves as they are – frightened children desperately trying to hide the truth from themselves and everybody else.

Less able to cope functionally are the multitudes of people who suffer from what is popularly called an inferiority complex. They feel inferior and are convinced that they are. It is all right, they argue, to talk in terms of self-value and personal worthfulness, but what about the individuals who have little or apparently nothing to commend them, most of all to themselves? They know what they are and genuinely believe themselves to be of poor value. Any talk of celebrating their selfhood is a joke in poor taste and clearly outside the bounds of serious consideration. That is how *they* feel, whatever the views of other people.

I have such persons in mind when I suggest that existing forms of church worship are sometimes more a hindrance than a help in encouraging worshippers to affirm their own identity and feel their own worth. Yet Christian fellowship at its best does strengthen, not weaken, selfhood and feed a person's sense of identity and value. It encourages a man not to grovel, but to stand on his own feet and look life in the eye; defeat his façade of self-importance by helping him to know himself, accept himself, and be himself. Yes, to be *himself*, not the caricature of an impossible ideal beyond his capacity.

What I am trying to say is that worship of God should also be the celebration of personal significance. Superficially, I realize, this concept appears to be self-contradictory. For is not the whole point of worship to forget oneself, one's habitual self-centredness, in contemplation of the creator, governor and protector of all things? From one standpoint it *is*, as many worshippers testify; but what of the others, those who find customary church services little more than an exercise in self-disparagement, an invitation to acknowledge that they are pathetically dependent, and an implicit suggestion that to try to be otherwise is somehow evidence of the sort of pride that goes before a fall, a real cropper – and serve you right too!

True enough, the spirit of worship incorporates a recognition of unworthiness, one that leads to penitence and forgiveness. Without encouraging unhealthy introspection and its crushing burden of guilt, it sometimes sharpens our insight into the nature of self-interest and thereby deepens both our consciousness of sin and our spirit of repentance. But at the same time, or automatically following on, worship of God results in the worshipper feeling that he is of value. There is little doubt, I imagine, that most people would agree that ideally worship is a celebration. The problem is that the form of

80

church celebration is losing its appeal, progressively, it seems, within the company of regular worshippers as well as those on the periphery of the church; and the reason, I think, is not only the various forms of celebration, the order of service we adopt, whatever our tradition, in our approach to worship.

We have already noticed that people generally in our secular society are finding the very idea of God increasingly difficult. What satisfied their forebears leaves them asking disturbing questions, questions fashioned on the anvil of secularization. One self-evident result is their growing tendency to reject institutional religion, but what about worship! Is that also being rejected or simply ignored? Thought of in traditional terms, the answer undoubtedly is *yes*. But what if, as well as saying that worship of God is a celebration of personal significance, we also say that a celebration of personal significance is worship of God. Are you prepared to consider this possibility?

There is no doubt that people do celebrate, in all sorts of ways and for all manner of reasons. This is one explanation, I believe, why they still call upon the church to mark births, weddings, and deaths. There are some sincere churchmen who resent this, claiming that such individuals are merely making a convenience of the church and practising not religion but a form of superstition. They probably have a point, but by no means the whole truth of the matter. I still believe that the church should minister to them in these ways if only because they are, I am convinced, seeking to celebrate, even paradoxically at a funeral. They want to affirm their own and other people's selfhood; give expression to their intuitive belief in the intrinsic value of human life.

Think, for a moment, of some of the ordinary ways in which people celebrate. A woman buys a new dress. Or she may change the one she is wearing once or twice a day. Why? She will tell you that it makes her *feel* good; gives her confidence and assurance. Never mind that possibly other people don't know or notice that she has changed her dress yet again or is wearing a new one. *She* knows and this makes all the difference in the world to how she feels. The same applies to her hair-do. It gives her confidence and helps her to relax in company. On the other hand, though her hair looks as lovely as ever, if she has not been to the hairdresser and suspects that she 'looks a fright' she will be anxious and semi-apologetic. Of course, there are women who do not worry how they look and pour scorn on those who do, thinking of them as vain or indulgent. They think of money spent at the hairdressers and the like as a waste and – the world being what it is in terms of human need – as unbecoming of responsible Christians. Obviously they are entitled to their opinion, but only if they do not express it to spread feelings of guilt and self-disregard. For people need to celebrate in ways that are meaningful to themselves, and many women clearly find that making the very best of their appearance is an affirmation of their selfhood. It can be argued that some women 'celebrate' not to affirm their selfhood, but to compensate for lack of it. I agree. The solution, however, is not to dismiss such celebrations as useless but rather to increase them; that is, to increase the number of occasions when personal significance is affirmed.

Men, too, celebrate both to affirm their selfhood and to compensate for lack of it. Few things are more pathetic than to see men trying to celebrate without having adequate selves to affirm or lacking the healthy self-respect of true individuality. Almost inevitably they are unnatural – drink too much, sing raucously or otherwise attract attention to themselves with the technique of extravagance; either this or the other extreme – self-consciously wallow in artificial jollity. Such celebrations fail because there is no *one* to celebrate, like a wedding without a bride, a Judy without a Punch, a person without a self. Other family and social reasons apart, this indicates why birthday celebrations, like parties of almost any kind, are so important. They help to affirm the selfhood of the persons or person being celebrated.

Perhaps one of the most telling revelations of what a person truly is is the object and nature of his celebrations, what and why he wants to celebrate. Some people, far from affirming themselves as real persons, persons of worth, use any form of celebration to escape from themselves; to forget and live in a fantasy world if only for a few hours. They are to be pitied, not ridiculed or patronized. Not a few of them hide their sense of non-identity and non-being by assuming the role of 'the life and soul of the party', but the empty noisiness of their laughter gives the game away, most of all to these inwardly wretched focal points of apparent fun. All the celebration in the world is poor compensation and does little or nothing to meet their basic need. Their artificial gaiety is a cry for someone to take them seriously, to treat them as persons of value for their own sake.

Possible ways of doing this are sometimes too self-evident to be noticed. A clasp of the hand, a smile, an expression of pleasure at meeting, a kiss, an embrace, a capacity to listen with single-mindedness, a word of encouragement or praise, a compliment or loving criticism; the list is endless and points to the essential requirement – authentic concern, spontaneous, sustained and sensitive. For people are not affirmed in their selfhood by being pampered or excused. They need far more than the sufferance of self-conscious charity. Ask the wife or husband whose partner mistakes words for deeds, identifies intentions with attitudes or makes promises without the costly commitment that often goes with them. They know the difference between being affirmed and feeling forsaken, forsaken within what otherwise looks like a happy marriage. They know that so often what we say with words is contradicted by our eyes; that the promises we keep are sometimes broken by the spirit motivating the deed; that the assurance of love is undermined by the tone of voice or the attitude of secret irritation. Children too are quick to notice or feel the difference. Their loneliness is not smothered by gifts or privileges any more than their sense of forsakenness is healed by preoccupied parents protesting their love.

Put simply and going to the heart of the matter, people are affirmed as persons primarily by the nature of their relationships. They feel of value only to the extent that they *are* truly valued by another. To say *that* is to underline the unhappy plight of many individuals. Within relationships of all sorts, some supposedly loving, others more impersonal and formal, they feel themselves dehumanized perhaps for no other reason than that they are never taken seriously. No one asks their opinion or if they do rarely takes any notice. They are used, even exploited, criticized, ignored, pushed aside (usually with fastidious politeness), spoken to only when they speak or somebody needs something, and generally made to feel of little or no account. Ironically, this happens not infrequently within situations of overt affection and spoken respect, which means that the people responsible are usually totally blind to what their indifference is doing within another person's life. The answer is not for the individuals concerned to go to church on Sunday. That might help; it certainly should, but something more is needed.

The first thing, I believe, is for the church to recognize and accept that the vast majority of people – and this is nothing new – will celebrate life, in so far as they celebrate life at all, outside the present ecclesiastical structures. For churchmen to feel guilt about this is as mistaken as, for instance, parents feeling guilty because their children think and function in ways different from their own. It is now generally acknowledged that the kingdom of God is not dependent upon how many people attend a place of worship. We recognize that God is at work far beyond the confines of the institutional church, an insight

84

which drives us to the conclusion that people can be outside the institution but inside the kingdom. There are mischievous commentators who even suggest that people can be inside the institution but outside the kingdom,' but such futile speculation leads only to the cul-de-sac of verbal warfare and confused meanings. We shall give it the attention it deserves.

More to the point is the exciting awareness that the church is the servant of the kingdom which incorporates the institution but is not restricted to it. Indeed, I would want to insist that, despite the distance we still have to go – and I have no wish to minimize that – society's growing concern for social justice, epitomized by the Welfare State, indicates the extent to which the Body of Christ has fulfilled the role of leaven, salt, and light. Far from decrying the so-called permissive and secular society, as distinct from certain aspects of its development, the church has every reason to rejoice that her influence in the world is bearing so much fruit. Who cares that the institutional church is being dismissed as irrelevant so long as the interests of the kingdom are being served? If churchmen themselves care, fussing over their concerns with the excitability of a hen rounding up her chicks for her peace of mind, not their safety, they should ponder again the words of Jesus about losing life (or even reputation) to find it.

In face of the continuing trend of the vast majority of people celebrating life outside the existing structures of organized religion, the church, it seems to me, has three areas of concern, each of them related to current emphases and priorities. First of all, she must *celebrate* her faith. Of course, the church believes in celebration, but even the clergy themselves – a brave band these days if ever there was one – hardly give the impression of going to a party as they tread towards morning or evening celebration. It is surely deplorable that so many faithful churchgoers are more bored than blessed by routine worship, and long for change; not the change that dismisses the familiar as useless or meaningless. What they want is simply to celebrate the gospel of Christ at the points of life that carry most meaning for them. Not for one moment do I expect every service to be exciting or out of the ordinary for everybody all the time. That would create other no less complex problems. But I do believe that generally speaking the element of celebration, which cannot, of course, be manufactured, has been forgotten or formalized beyond easy recognition.

The main reason is, I believe, that we are rather confused about what it is we are supposedly celebrating. Words have replaced experience and ceremonial has been substituted for reality. There are no elementary or quick remedies, but I feel constrained to make the suggestion that we should spend more time together exploring what it is in our corporate experience that we believe warrants and demands celebration. The answer to dullness in worship lies, I think, more in a new theology than in new methods, no matter how bold the experimentation. It certainly cannot be denied that all manner of experiments are taking place with liturgy and other forms of worship, details of which are readily available.[1]

However, my immediate concern is to ask that our worship of God should also be a celebration of man; that it should enhance the worshippers, affirm their selfhood, and by the very nature of their acknowledgment of dependence upon God deepen their sense of responsible independence. This element of dependence-independence is an essential oscillation of life, whether people believe in God or not. At times we all need to feel dependent, to be aware that there is someone upon whom we can rely without fear or reservation. To be driven into a position of unrelieved fiery independence or to mistake such an attitude as evidence of maturity is to be impoverished and unbalanced. Yet there is a difference between dependence and humiliating subservience, a difference which sometimes

86

appears to be overlooked in some of the church's traditional liturgical expressions. Reflecting alien societies and cultural patterns, these tend to portray God as 'the big boss', ignoring the way our society's attitude to big bosses of every kind has changed. Ordinary people no longer touch their caps either in fact or in spirit as the modern counterpart of the lord of the manor passes in all his self-importance. They might well have respect, but do not feel subservient; and their respect has to be earned. It flows spontaneously out of their perception that the person concerned is *worth* respecting. The same applies to their attitude to authority and authorities of whatever kind. There was a time when a man or group of men exercised authority simply because of personal status as reflected in position and prestige, but other factors now predominate. Positions of authority are not entirely ignored, but the holders speak with authority primarily to the extent that their authority is intrinsic to themselves. Inevitably there are bosses in modern society, but they exercise authority as partners in a shared enterprise. Once they try to lord it over their fellows they meet with resistance and encourage at least verbal warfare.

Now it seems to me that the church, understandably from some standpoints, continues to represent God as the boss to whom one never answers back or even privately questions his dictates. I realize that to think of God as more partner than boss does seem to some people both irreverent and near sacrilegious. But would they think of, say, an independent man's relationship with his father as necessarily less respectful than the one he had as a child? Rather couldn't it be argued that the element of partnership was essential before the relationship could reach its maximum fulfilment? The father and son would accept each other with mutual love and respect, and this, other considerations apart, would affirm for each of them their individuality and self-value. Neither the father nor the son would wish to impose upon the other or infringe the other's freedom to be a real person. Such respect bordering on reverence would not resolve necessarily every disagreement or result in the two men holding views or sharing activity which pleased them both equally, but it would make their every meeting a celebration, for their togetherness would affirm their personal significance. The last thing either of them would wish would be to rub the other's nose in the mud of guilt, self-disparagement, morbid introspection, or the things we all too readily associate with worship of God.

This leads me to another major element in customary Christian worship, one I have hinted at before. Rightly understood it adds to the spirit of celebration and thereby helps the worshipper to grow, but at the moment it seems primarily to underline his worthlessness and wrong doing. He is a sinner. More to the point, he is either a miserable sinner or a sort of castrated saint. Some of my ecclesiastical friends assure me that miserable means pitiable, but this hardly helps as far as I am concerned. The whole liturgical exercise seems centred upon persuading the worshippers to be sorry for being themselves. They should, in the name of penitence or humility, preferably both, confess their shortcomings and promise to try harder to overcome all the dreadful impulses which make up their personalities or simple humanity. Intended or otherwise, the result encourages them not only to confess their sins, but to despise themselves as sinners.

There are sincere believers who think that this is as it should be. After all, they argue, people of whatever kind *are* sinners and need to see themselves in this light, otherwise they cannot receive forgiveness and be reconciled to God. The trouble, as I see it, is that these good people, forgiven and reconciled, then feel less than themselves or afraid to be themselves. It is surely significant that in all the records of Jesus' involvement with 'publicans and sinners' there is not the slightest suggestion that he emphasized their wickedness or ever drew

88

attention to their numerous failings. Clearly he knew that condemnation, like ritualized affirmation of personal worthlessness,
was destructive and finally futile. This does not mean that he
under-estimated the lethal nature of sin or condoned its practice. But it does indicate that true penitence is impossible
outside the context of love and total acceptance. It is when
a man knows himself to be loved like that, loved without
condition or variation, that he begins to understand and
experience the nature of penitence. And his confession of
sin, far from pushing him further into the abyss of self-
despising if not despair, liberates him to become more fully
himself. The operation – and sometimes it does feel like major
surgery – is often seen in human relationships. A child, knowing himself loved despite his wrong doing, apologizes with
tears and perhaps not a little distress, but his awareness of still
being accepted as a person by his parents, against whom
possibly he has offended, restores for him a broken relationship with them and encourages his own self-acceptance. Their
attitude of forgiveness neither demands a detailed recital of
the offence nor demeans the boy as an individual in his own
eyes. On the contrary, their forgiveness, probably deepening
his penitence, actually affirms his identity and self-worth, and
also stiffens his resolve to be worthy of their love and his own
self-respect which their love gives to him.

In this sense, confession of wrong doing is a celebration of
the love that accepts unconditionally and the personal value
such love ascribes to the sinner. Yet how mournful we sometimes make our approach to God in formal worship. It is
almost as though we were not sure of our acceptance and felt
the need to emphasize our wickedness as proof of our sincerity.
I certainly get the impression that some of us imagine that God
responds only to the degree that we confess our chronic
dependence, and this, no matter what pious words we utter,
is neither true to our way of life nor an accurate reflection of

our real feelings. Little wonder, then, that worship seems unrelated to reality and degenerates for many people into tedious obligation.

However, what we must go on to ask is how the church, having re-discovered the meaning of celebration and fashioned ways to express it in contemporary form, can help the growing number of people outside her structures to do likewise. If you insist that the only reason to celebrate is faith in God and the Lord Jesus Christ, in those precise terms, then clearly you must stick to your guns and work out your convictions. I ask only for the freedom to do the same.

Apart from celebrating her faith in routine worship, the church should celebrate *before* the world. There is hardly anything surprising or revolutionary about that! Yet I wonder. Is it true that in every expression of her life and witness, the church encourages people to feel of value? Whatever your answer, there is no doubt that all of us should help each other and the people we meet in the course of daily life to feel significant and of worth. I believe that we have failed in no greater way. Indeed, I believe that the Body of Christ has sometimes turned the means of grace within her care into the ends of disgrace for innumerable people. We have politely persecuted each other in the name of devout exhortation, and separated ourselves from each other in the name of doctrinal conviction or even personal holiness. My argument is simply that if association with us does not *enhance* people, whether they be loved ones, friends or whoever, we are not celebrating the gospel in the spirit of Jesus of Nazareth.

The sort of celebration I have in mind extends far beyond the confines of organized religion. It is expressed in our brief encounters with bus conductors, shop assistants, street sweepers, postmen, hawkers, and many others. Ideally the tone of our life, wholly unconscious, affirms their selfhood, our attitude of reverence (I am being really idealistic now) gives them a lift for reasons beyond their immediate knowing. But that is what celebration is all about, as we recognize from our encounters with people who make us feel good and inspire us to want to be good. Of course, it is far easier, and for many of us more pleasant, to worship God in supposed spiritual terms, confessing our sins and singing our praises within a consecrated building. And I have no complaint about such exercises, wanting to share them myself, but far from being incompatible with the kind of celebration I have suggested they ideally prompt it and help to sustain it in moments of personal stress and irritation.

The church also celebrates life before the world in her fight for social justice. Her concern is to safeguard human dignity. Of all institutions the Body of Christ knows that if any area of human experience makes celebration impossible or more difficult it is plainly contrary to the will of God and an affront to the humanity of those involved. Where the celebration of life, therefore, is stifled by poor housing, poverty, inadequate schooling, racism, and other forms of deprivation often legitimized by brutal laws, the voice of the church is heard and part of her own celebrating of the gospel is her costly involvement with the victims concerned. To celebrate in any other way is to mistake the sacred for the profane, and to trivialize God in the sight of men.

This leads me to the third trend I want to see encouraged. I believe that the church should concentrate much more on celebrating *with* the world. By 'the world' I mean, of course, people. There was a time, notably in the Puritan tradition, when involvement in the world – simply with unconverted people – was thought to detract from the authority of the believer's personal testimony. Such ideas are no longer prevalent, but one hangover from this sort of thinking is the assumption, or at least suspicion, that celebration outside the church is necessarily different in kind from celebration within.

The two are thought to be fundamentally at variance and probably contradictory. But are they? We have already seen that true celebration results in people feeling affirmed in their selfhood and their sense of personal worth. This sometimes happens when believers approach God according to church traditions, but it no less happens when people, believers in God or not, share an occasion of celebration. The emphasis is, I believe, basically the same, though clearly the motivation is different. But is the reality being celebrated so very different, for in essence any activity that enhances people and humanizes society is a celebration of love, which surely suggests that God, however conceptualized, is at the centre. There is no doubt that though the vast majority of people know little or nothing of systems of worship, certainly within organized religion, they know plenty about the spirit of wonder; and in so far as so-called non-religious men and women are gripped by that spirit they are, I believe, sharing the attitude to which Jesus of Nazareth referred when he talked about the need to become as little children. He knew that life tended to make people hard-boiled and cynical; that hurtful experiences of disillusionment fostered within them the spirit of sophistication and prompted the search for ulterior motivation behind every appearance of goodness. Little children, on the other hand, are full of wonder because they are empty of pretentiousness; *little* children! All too soon youngsters learn the art of diplomacy and subterfuge. They pick up the 'wisdom' of being phoney, of saying the right thing out of scheming intention, with at least one eye on the main chance. There is nothing deliberately vicious or selfish in such an approach. It is thought of in terms of being worldly-wise, facing stern reality in an affluent society, of oiling the wheels of personal relationships. The aim is not so much to exploit as to please or endear, and frequently the aim is achieved. But never more than superficially, which is the measure of all too many relationships, even those supposedly open and intimate. This is sad enough, as stale flippancy often illustrates, but worse still is the way childlike wonder surrenders to suspicion and the unrealized acceptance of drabness. Few individuals, it seems, theists and non-theists alike, manage to maintain their zest for living even until, let alone beyond, their years of adolescence. They exist rather than live and yawn their way from one miracle to another. The process is sometimes called 'growing up', ceasing to be starry-eyed, or some similarly misleading rationalization.

The fact is that when a man loses his capacity for wonder he begins to die within himself. He looks and sees nothing, listens and hears only noise, touches and does not feel, tastes and concentrates on the next mouthful. His preoccupation with 'reality' sets him in the direction of being artificial, of sustaining life with ever more ingenious synthetic products. The irony is that even religion, its symbols and observances, its worship and celebration, sometimes takes the sparkle out of life and drains it of wonder. Not always, by a long way; only sometimes. And this leads me to reiterate that religion in essence or faith in God is not a question of this or that orthodox belief, but of having a religious attitude to life, one of wondering openness and gratitude.

NOTE

1. See, for instance, John Killinger, *Leave it to the Spirit*, SCM Press 1971.

6

The Saviourhood of Christ[1]

Times without number I have heard devout Christians say or sing: 'When you call him Saviour, you call him by his name.' Now there's no doubt that such affirmations of faith issue from living experience. The people I have in mind testify to the reality of Christ in their lives. He is the indwelling presence who makes their whole existence meaningful, the one who transforms the drabness and even the disasters of human experience into the service of goodness. In that sense he is the redeemer, for nothing is beyond his power to redeem. All things, whatever their nature, work together for good, and they do so because finally everything is subservient to the fulfilment of his purposes.

However, it is equally certain that secular man finds such thinking, let alone its vocabulary, utterly meaningless and, worse still, superfluous. He does not want to argue about 'God by some other name' if only because God himself, thought to be redundant, is acknowledged by nothing more than a polite nod or more probably is dismissed by an attitude of unthinking indifference. What chance, then, have such people of knowing the Saviourhood of Christ?

There are churchmen who say that to be saved a man must believe what Jesus believed about God, but for me at least this creates one or two major problems. First of all, I am not sure that we know, or ever can know, precisely what Jesus believed about God. Some of us, it is true, give the impression that we know it all. We talk about the teaching of Jesus and the traditions of the church as though everything was so self-evident. 'The Bible *says* . . .', we declare, apparently forgetting that other equally dedicated men and women, reading the same verses, come to a different – perhaps fundamentally different – interpretation of what the Bible *means*. Of course, it is possible for us to insist that our interpretation is infallibly correct – or at least more infallibly correct than anyone else's! – in which case we should not get so hot under the collar when the Pope, with *ex cathedra* pronouncements in mind, makes the same claim. But the essential problem remains: what exactly did Jesus of Nazareth say and mean? Dogmatism at this point is the death-knell for truth and precludes, I believe, even the possibility of God revealing further light from his word.

But apart from the difficulty of knowing precisely what Jesus believed about God, the next problem is no less complex: are we saying, supposing that we could know with greater certainty what Jesus believed about God, that he is known as Saviour only in theological terms, meaning of course *our* theological terms? If that sounds facetious I've probably given the right impression. My concern, however, is to focus what for some of us is a crucial question, an area of enquiry which sometimes within organized religion appears to bristle with over-simple answers to matters of profound human experience.

This could explain in part why the church is no longer credible for so many people in our secular society. And by 'secular' I simply mean a society in which life is organized without conscious reference to God or institutional religion. One aspect of this trend is that more and more people are not asking the questions for which we believe we have the answers. There is no doubt that if only they would ask the questions we should have something useful to say. But they will not or at least they do not. Of course, a shrinking minority do and often find our answers convincing to the point of seeking to be initiated into our sort of experience of God in Christ. That minority is important and obviously should remain one focal point of the church's ministry. But what about all the other people for whom our answers are 'incredible' for no other reason than that they are not asking the questions we insist on answering? Have we nothing to say to them until they *do* begin to ask the 'right' questions and also of necessity learn our vocabulary in order to understand the mysteries of our answers?

Some sincere Christians believe that this is the only way forward: that the church, whatever the reaction of unbelievers and disbelievers, must continue to declare her message and practise her faith in accredited words and ways. I cannot believe that this concept of the gospel represents a monopoly of truth. It undoubtedly represents truth for the people who believe it, but not for everybody, either inside or more particularly outside the institutional church. So what is the gospel? In what sense, if any, is Christ the Saviour for men who do not believe?

There are evangelicals who give, it seems to me, the impression that Christ is Saviour only for the weak. The supposition is that he reaches out a rescuing arm to inadequate personalities, people like alcoholics, chronic depressives, drug abusers and addicts of various kinds, the fearful and guilt-ridden, the rejects of society whose weakness of will appears to be built into their fundamental make-up. To call Christ Saviour in such situations is immediately intelligible. But what about the strong? It can be argued that no one *is* strong; that we are all weak in degree. The only difference is how the weakness is revealed – or perhaps camouflaged by respectability and fastidious attention to appearances. This is, I believe, an over-simplication that will not bear examination in the light of some people's experience; but no matter! We are still left trying to understand the Saviourhood of Christ for people who appear to cope without being saved, at least saved in the traditional meaning of that word within the institutional church. Is it possible for Christ to become their Saviour in any meaningful way?

To get at the answer we must first of all obviously consider the person of Christ himself. Who was he and what essentially was his mission? Christians have claimed, of course, that he was God or the Son of God or God in the flesh. The terms vary a little, but not to the extent of changing their fundamental meaning. However, what do they convey not only to people who find God-talk largely beside the point, if not positively boring, but also to believers within the church?

God in the flesh! It is hardly surprising that such words do no more than indicate rather than define the reality they symbolize. How could it be otherwise? Yet still some of us, anxious to defend the Christian faith as we understand it, are inclined to dogmatize about exactly how God became flesh, getting ourselves embroiled in arguments about the pre-existent Christ with verbal imagery which suggests a sort of moon shot in reverse. If you insist that this is not the case, I can only say that your experience in talking to believers within the institutional church and rank outsiders is different from mine.

As far as Jesus of Nazareth is concerned, the claim that he was God in the flesh is often understood to imply that he had the attributes of God. He was, for instance, omniscient, *all*-knowing. But clearly he was not. Like all of us, he was a child of his age, limited in his understanding of knowledge since opened up by man's insatiable search for truth. Beyond doubt he knew less about the universe than Copernicus and Galileo, less about physics than Albert Einstein, less about nuclear fission than Robert Oppenheimer, less about heart transplants than Christian Barnard. Forgive me for illustrating my point so crudely, but it seems the only way to correct an impression – indeed, a conviction – I have met time and again in conversation with all manner of people. Many of them, devout and uncompromising in their Christian commitment, appear to believe, judging by their sometimes incensed reaction, that to suggest that Jesus of Nazareth was not all-knowing about everything is somehow to undermine the traditional claims made about him by historic Christianity.

Likewise it needs to be said, I think, that Jesus of Nazareth was not omnipotent, *all*-powerful. Often he was weary to the point of exhaustion, a peculiar condition for omnipotent man. He needed to eat and sleep, to replenish his spent energy in prayer and relaxation. There were occasions when he was hindered in his healing ministry by other people's lack of faith, and made the victim of power wielded by representatives of civic and ecclesiastical government. In the light of all this, to say that Jesus, being God, was all-powerful is to ignore the facts and to make pious words a cover for paucity of thought.

Whatever we think of Jesus of Nazareth being all-knowing and all-powerful, there can be no argument that, unlike God as traditionally conceptualized, he was not omnipresent, everywhere present. Like all of us, he was restricted to one place at one time. If he was with his disciples in Galilee he could not be with other of his disciples simultaneously in Judaea. Now I know that all this is straightforward enough, but the peculiar thing is that it creates such controversy among the faithful. They hate to acknowledge that Jesus, being God or God in the flesh, was not omniscient and omnipotent; and they are quick to explain that although clearly he was not omnipresent during his earthly life, he undoubtedly became so immediately after the resurrection. On the other hand, many church leaders are happy to give the assurance that the ideas we have been considering have nothing to do with the essential meaning of God in the flesh in the first place. Such ideas, they insist, are childish and unrelated to sound doctrinal teaching. They explain that Jesus of Nazareth was God in the sense that he was the fullest revelation in human terms of ultimate reality.

Without lingering to ask what *that* means, I can only comment that faced by questions already asked in previous chapters – What person or group of persons has apprehended the *full* revelation of God? If the revelation was so apprehended why do responsible church leaders differ so basically about its meaning, for contemporary society? – the situation, far from being clarified, is made more obscure than ever. Much of the confusion, it seems to me, follows from the use of such words as divine and perfect. We say that Jesus of Nazareth was divine, and wonder why so many people, notably those not versed in theology, are baffled. For what do we mean? That we mean something, and something undoubtedly important is beyond dispute, but is there really no other way of making the point? Must we continue to evoke disharmony and bewilderment by using words which, if at one time intelligible to our forebears in the faith and even people generally, are now evidently more emotive than enlightening? My concern, like yours, is to safeguard and share the good news of Christ, but this, as we know from hard experience, involves far more than defending time-honoured words, which we agree, some of us strictly privately, are no longer adequate to communicate what we believe.

Perhaps this dilemma – and to under-estimate its complexity helps no one – is seen nowhere more sharply than in our customary insistence that Jesus of Nazareth was perfect. But simply to ask in what sense he was perfect man is to expose some of the profound difficulties. Perfect man! The very notion is self-contradictory for most people. If he was perfect, they argue, he was not a man; if he was a man he was not perfect. It is as plain as that. Our immediate reaction, those of

99

us who believe that Jesus was unique, is to start to explain what we do not mean when we say that he was perfect. He certainly was not perfect in knowledge, as we have already noticed. Neither was he perfect in ability, as though anything we can do he could do better. Such an assumption is, of course, speculative, no more, and almost certainly not the case. Maybe he was a perfect carpenter, though this in itself is highly debatable, but there is no reason to believe that he was even capable of being, say, the perfect architect or artist. Was he a potential Picasso, Beethoven, Shakespeare, and (shall we say) Yehudi Menuhin rolled into one? Does belief in his perfection mean that everything he did was done perfectly and also that everything anyone else has done he could have done better? This is clearly the viewpoint of many devout Christians, but I for one find the idea incredible.

Ah, yes, say some scholars and other commentators, but this is not what perfect means in this case. He was perfect man, was Jesus of Nazareth, in the sense that he was morally perfect; knew perfectly right from wrong and always did the right thing perfectly. I get the distinction, but remain no less confused. Is the claim to be taken seriously that Jesus never made a mistake? What about his choice of Judas? Was that not a mistake of judgment? If I prayerfully selected a man to support what I believed to be the most important cause in the world and he turned out to be a traitor I should find it hard to pretend that there was not something fundamentally wrong with my initial judgment. Yet such considerations apart, what I am really asking is whether the words *perfect man* as traditionally interpreted within the teaching of the church can ever have real meaning for us. There are people who insist that perfect in this context is synonymous with sinless; and they go on, not only to invite us to believe that Jesus of Nazareth was a sinless man, but also a sinless boy. Imagine – a sinless *boy*! The mind boggles. What sort of grotesque non-person are we trying to foist upon the minds of ordinary people in our attempts rightly to claim that Jesus of Nazareth was unique, the very fulness of the Godhead *bodily*? I sometimes wonder whether the parrot-fashion repetition of phrases beloved of some churchmen is deemed more important than a living encounter with the truths they imperfectly represent.

Needless to say, I am not asking that we should stop believing that Jesus of Nazareth was both perfect and sinless. My concern is to ask what such terms mean for us, committed Christians, who believe that we have the treasure of the kingdom and want not only progressively to appropriate its riches, but also to share our good fortune. For surely only to the extent that we understand our own terms are we likely to be able to communicate what we are trying to say! Personally I find the concept of sinlessness both unintelligible and unnecessary. Jesus *was* perfect, but only in the sense, I believe, that he was the perfect fulfilment of himself, Jesus of Nazareth. He fulfilled perfectly his own potential as a man; did the work that God gave *him* to do. As no one else, it seems to me, he was able to say at the end of his life: 'It is finished', and to say it in terms that cannot be mistaken – at the place where he proved his love for God and man. At the cross I begin to understand what suffering is all about and somehow, quite independently of whether Jesus was a sinless boy or not, whatever that means, I am aware of ultimate meaning. It hinges for me upon the insight that, first and foremost, the quality of life to which we have referred, that inward richness which incorporates the mystical and the mysterious, is related to the open secret of Jesus of Nazareth's perfection – the perfect fulfilment of himself as an authentic person. Such a concept of perfection is the very opposite of the caricature to which our minds have sometimes been directed – a man infallibly correct about everything and incapable of thinking or doing less than the absolute ideal.

Too many of us, I fear, despite our commendable zeal, seek to be other than ourselves. We become idolaters at the altar of perfectionism, the minimum standard to which we feel ourselves called and committed. The inescapable consequence is that we become not more but less whole; more frantic and less authentic. Guilt, morbidity, self-alienation, destructive tension, and much else suggestive of an unbalanced attitude to life are rarely outside our experience.

There is something else too that many believers mean when they talk about Jesus the perfect Saviour. They are really referring to a distinctive style of life in which Jesus is central and which spells out the perfect solution to every conceivable problem. To them the all-important question is: what would Jesus do? It never occurs to them that God does not want us to do what Jesus did. He wants us to do what we, distinctive individuals, should do. In other words, he wants us to *be* ourselves, to fulfil our own potential as persons in our own right and not slavishly emulate an example for ever beyond our capacity. Countless believers, many of them the very 'salt of the earth', invite misery and frustration into their lives by demanding of themselves impossible standards and achievements in the name of God. By the nature of things they fail repeatedly and are then tempted to indulge in self-condemnation and futile regret.

Some of us know the unhappiness of being inspired with our one talent to live as people with ten talents; or even with only five or two! With laudable if misguided zeal, we try to out-do our personalities and capacities, and succeed most of all in becoming little more than a trial to the people nearest at hand. We also become a frightful burden to ourselves. Despite our prayers and the grace of God, we know more of depression than the abundant life of our expectations and hopes. Admittedly I am stating the position in extreme terms; the reality is less clear-cut with an overlap of fluctuating depression and spasmodic Christian hilarity, but the emphasis illustrates the meaning I am after.

These considerations apart, what we have to recognize is that so often, at those points of life that concern us most, we simply do not know what Jesus of Nazareth would have done. He lived in an agricultural society, ours is technological; in his society the existence of God was axiomatic, in our society secularization is operative not least in the realm of organized religion, and tending sometimes to give way to secularism; in his day responsible self-assertion was identified with the defiance of God, in ours it is often interpreted as praiseworthy evidence of self-value and growing maturity. With such fundamental changes to society's thinking and structures it is hardly surprising that many of the questions confronting us are not mentioned in the New Testament.

We do not know, for instance, what Jesus would do about abortion, euthanasia, war, divorce, contraception, the re-marriage of divorcees in church, and much else. Of course, we have our opinions, even our dogmatic convictions, but these frequently contradict each other, not least when voiced by responsible church leaders. The question of whether or not to strike further underlines the difficulties of knowing what Jesus would do in our complex society. Beyond argument the principle of industrial action is now accepted by virtually everybody, employer and employee alike, but this does not alter or resolve the dilemma in which many dedicated Christians find themselves. Called out on strike (if not members of the executive group which initiates the call) they wonder about their prior commitment and wrestle with their consciences as to where their first loyalty lies. Some of them decide one thing, some another. All of them approach the situation as Christians and seek sincerely to interpret their responsibilities in such terms. They pray, seek the guidance of the Holy Spirit, possibly consult their priest or minister, and otherwise try to discern the will of God. But still they are incapable of knowing with anything like unanimity what Jesus would do in their immediate circumstances.

There are few, if any, categoric answers. It is not the function of the Bible to provide them anyway. The Bible provides answers only by helping us to ask the right questions and to wrestle with them in the light of biblical perspective; that is, the whole Bible's whole view of the whole of life – hardly a minor undertaking for the manufacture of ready-made answers. Once this is overlooked or its complexity underestimated, dogmatic conclusions reveal a devout and usually unconscious development which issues in a God made in the image of man. By such devious means the question *what would Jesus do?* is answered in terms of what I think Jesus should have done. And the answer is not usually a dodge to escape the moral challenge of Christ, the very opposite. More often it reflects a closed mind's assumption that Jesus always denied himself to the degree of never saying *yes* to his personal desires, interests, pleasures, needs. Never! For anything nice (enjoyable), it is confidently assumed, is wrong or at least highly suspicious. No wonder that in such circumstances Jesus is Saviour in name only, for he seems utterly incapable of saving our situation and personality.

Now the root meaning of salvation is wholeness; to be made whole or to have one's face turned in that direction. Unfortunately this does not get us very far, if only because the essential meaning of wholeness, of what it means to be a whole person, is still obscure. Many of us believe that the central character of the four gospels was *whole*, but this does not necessarily help us to know what wholeness means for ourselves individually. If it did, those of us who follow Christ would reflect his wholeness to a greater degree. But even though we cannot analyse what it means to be a whole person in terms acceptable to everyone or in terms which, if accepted by everyone, would result inevitably in his becoming a whole person, we can point to Jesus of Nazareth as indicating what we mean by wholeness. He came, he himself said, that men might have *life* in all its fulness; and the abundance of that life he consistently exemplified. The secret of that richness of life is variously understood, even within the institution of the church, but there is an aspect of it which all sorts of people, I believe, are discovering for themselves. It is the insight that in the final analysis being true to one's deepest convictions, the ones hammered out on the anvil of experience, is the only way of salvation for any of us. That there are real dangers goes without saying, especially if we live in arrogant isolation and ignore the guidelines implicit in our traditions and culture, but the fact remains that wholeness is essentially related to a man's inner life; his response to truth, the nature of his commitment to goodness in love.

Now all this, I recognize, sounds vague and open to abuse, even to serious misjudgment and the painful consequences that go with it, but what is the alternative? There are churchmen who like to equate truth with orthodox belief, as though to believe the teaching of the institutional church is the same as knowing the truth and therefore of moving in the direction of wholeness. This, however, is clearly not the case. The German church of the thirties was orthodox enough in its doctrinal teaching. Devout churchmen of South Africa and the Bible belt of the USA subscribe whole-heartedly to the central affirmations of Christianity, but this doesn't save them from racism. A book published in 1970 – *Almost All are Welcome*[2] – tells the story of a Baptist church in the USA, one which prided itself on its biblical preaching and evangelical outreach. I repeat the main points here not to indict, but to illustrate. A near-by university decided upon racial integration and the minister of the church wanted his congregation to do likewise. He called the deacons together, but they could not agree. A new element of urgency was introduced into the already tense atmosphere when black worshippers, encouraged by the example of the university and mistaking this for a more liberal policy everywhere, began to arrive at the church. Finally the congregation, not without acrimony, voted against integration and dismissed the minister.

One of the men excluded from worship was a student won to Christianity in Africa by missionaries financed by that same Baptist chuch. Now we all know that this spirit is not restricted to an isolated church of any particular denomination. It is not even typical, though in certain parts of the world, as we have seen, it is prevalent, not without terrible distress to some Christians in those areas. However, all I want to underline is that orthodox belief – and we have seen this time and again throughout this book – is no guarantee of wholeness for the believers. It is possible for people sincerely to believe the teaching of the church and remain sick in soul. Other factors are involved, some of which we have already considered; but there are others to which we have still to turn our attention. Meanwhile what I am anxious not to do is give the impression that orthodox belief, far from setting the believer's feet firmly on the way of wholeness, positively encourages *un*wholeness. Unfortunately sometimes this appears to be the case, and the appearance is neither easily penetrated nor its influence dispersed. In itself this makes the meaning I want to convey difficult to focus without distortion.

Charles Davis, who resigned from the priesthood in protest against what he called the 'corruption' of the Roman Catholic church, said in a talk broadcast on Radio Three and subsequently published in *The Listener*:

> Despite many writings and utterances with appropriate, forward-looking sentiments, the average congregation remains enclosed within a narrow moral code, unable to see the inadequacy of its morality or to regard any departure from it

as other than sin. Many Christians are refusing the drive towards transcendent value because in our present situation it urges them on beyond the familiar, the comfortable, the safe. The churches encourage their refusal because, for all the fine words, they are afraid of moral nakedness. They will not strip themselves of their traditional clothing in a creative movement towards a more suitable garb.[3]

This, I believe, is well said and points in the general direction of truth; but it is not the whole truth. For the churches also stand for the dimension of human experience which is crucial to our understanding of what it means to be a whole person. There is ecclesiastical confusion, incompetence, possible abuse, and even corruption; this cannot be denied. Yet within the guidelines of the church – of orthodox belief, if you like – countless people are sure that they are on to the means of their own identity as authentic persons. But they are authentic only to the degree that they follow truth as *they* perceive it, inspired, stimulated and mutually corrected by fellow-believers.

In this, of course, Jesus of Nazareth shows us the way. He was not play-acting when he cried: 'Why have you deserted me?' The question re-echoed terrible doubt and throbbed in his mind, challenging his defiance of traditional ideas and customs. At the same time it expressed the anguish of his loving concern that so many good and simple people were bewildered by his apparent unreasonableness in refusing to take greater cognizance of their conventional ways. Did the thought never cross his mind that he might be mistaken in going his own way, which, by the very nature of things, would make his own execution, he realized, virtually certain? Was he so free of doubts and questions, so sure all the time that he was right, infallibly so?

I cannot believe so, but what matters is that Jesus remained true to himself, to his own ultimate concerns. Whatever the price, he refused to compromise there; and people who do likewise are moving towards the wholeness of which he was the incarnation. They are asserting their responsible independence and discovering at depth the nature of freedom – the freedom of the sons and daughters of God. Significantly a growing number of them do not verbalize their discoveries in religious terms, but what they are saying – if we listen – is in perfect harmony with the insights and emphases of Jesus of Nazareth. Far from denying his Saviourhood, they are testifying that only when life is ordered by his evaluations and lived in his spirit does it serve the purposes of wholeness. Their experience is summarized by Monica Furlong in her book *Contemplating Now*: 'Christ is the human experience seen in action, as it were, and even if we do not begin to share conventional Christian belief, we may perhaps recognize similarity of the Christ-experience to states of mind that we have undergone, and which we have seen others undergo.'[4] In that sense, Christ is, I believe, the key to wholeness, the means whereby we come alive before we die, for Christians and non-Christians alike.

To approach the matter from a different standpoint, such people perceive that fundamental to life is a pattern of resurrection; that the rhythm of birth, death, resurrection is intrinsic somehow to the cosmos itself, to how life works, with the result that wholeness or the full life is brought nearer wherever men recognize this pattern or rhythm of resurrection and order their lives accordingly. This is one reason why, for instance, the cross of Christ is profoundly significant in religious and so-called secular terms. If I believe that Jesus of Nazareth was uniquely the Son of God then clearly my interpretation of his death will reflect the teaching of the church, though we should again note that such teaching has varied considerably and still does within the Christian tradition. But if I do not believe, the death of Christ still has profound meaning, epitomizing as it does the eternal struggle between good and evil, the possibility of triumph at the heart of tragedy, the nature of authority and

power, the meaning and cost of personal integrity, the related-
ness of self-sacrifice and self-fulfilment, the character of love's
conquest, and the vindication of crucified truth.

These realities are shared by everybody who is sensitive to
the tensions at the heart of life and who seeks to explore the
meaning of being a whole person, of becoming truly human, of
being saved or knowing the salvation experience. But they are
shared and their meaning explored in real-life, not theological,
terms. This is not to disparage theology. For some of us it is
important in helping us to understand our expanding self-
awareness and to contemplate what life is basically all about.
But the signs are that for most people, certainly a growing
number, it is considered a hindrance, apart from being a bore,
and is written off as being totally unrelated to the real issues
of human experience. All I am saying is that for many people
both inside and outside the church the new touchstone of truth
– that is, the truth about the world within ourselves – is, as we
noted earlier, not orthodoxy or authoritative pronouncements
of any kind, but experiential knowledge: does it work for me?;
does it help me to become a real person? All manner of
authorities can be consulted and their counsel possibly acted
upon, but *finally*, let me repeat, such questions can be answered
by no one but ourselves. We listen, discuss, ponder, look at
life from this aspect and that, experiment with due regard to
the integrity and intrinsic value of other people, keep probing
and prodding, but in the end we truly believe only what we
prove as real for ourselves. So Carl Jung, asked whether he
believed in the existence of God, replied: 'I do not believe, I
know.' In the realm of faith there is a point at which theological,
philosophical and other academic considerations, without in
any way losing their significance, are transcended by experiential knowledge. Notice the word: they are *transcended*, not
superseded. The distinction is important. At that point a
man believes on a new level. He might still cry: 'Lord, I

believe, help Thou my unbelief,'[5] but his plea is the longing of *un*satisfaction, not *dis*satisfaction, with the beyond-doubt reality of his existing experience of faith.

Perhaps I can further indicate what I mean when I say that most people are seeking the meaning of wholeness in real-life and not theological terms by looking once more at the cross of Christ. The Christian says: 'I believe in the atonement,' and usually he knows in essence what he means. But an increasing number of individuals in our secular society, as doubtless we have discovered in our personal conversations, are baffled by such terminology. The atonement! What in the world does that mean? And even if they wait for an answer, which is doubtful, they find reference to an event of almost 2,000 years ago enough to confirm their often unthinking assumption that institutional religion is unrelated to the affairs of this life, the here and now of real concerns. The fact remains, however, that they believe implicitly, if not in *the* atonement, certainly in atonement. Life itself has taught them that without the spirit of at-one-ment, with all that it implies of penitence, apology, forgiveness, reconciliation, restitution, unconditional acceptance, and suffering love, human relationships break down or never develop. I know some married couples, for instance – and so must you – whose growing relationship is characterized by atonement, the gentle spirit of at-one-ment. But in some cases talk of *the* atonement leaves them cold; it is neither welcome nor intelligible. Nevertheless are they not testifying as they work out their relationship that the essential meaning of *the* atonement is the key to all human relationships?

We can seek the answer to this question from yet another standpoint altogether. In his book *The Integrity of the Personality*, Anthony Storr observes: 'To know that another person accepts one just as one is, unconditionally, is to be able to accept oneself, and therefore to be able to *be* oneself, to realize one's own potential.'[6] Now a not inconsiderable number of people still find the freedom of self-acceptance in the realization that they are accepted unconditionally by God. This is their belief and faith, the means of their deliverance from the old life of self-rejection and frequent despair. They know themselves loved and affirmed in their selfhood. In the light of that undeniable fact – undeniable, that is, as far as they are concerned – they find it possible to accept themselves to the degree of asserting their highest potential and constantly, if spasmodically, moving towards its greater fulfilment. But far more people experience self-acceptance through a human relationship of unconditional acceptance. They know themselves loved in a way that is not contingent upon their apparent worth or their proving themselves worthy. They are simply – and incredibly – loved for themselves alone. Though the sky fall, they know beyond doubt that nothing could destroy the love of which they are the focal point. Such unconditional acceptance by another person knows nothing of condoning personal indulgence or turning a blind eye to unnecessary mediocrity. It is not afraid to challenge and rebuke. At the same time its very *againstness* communicates the depth of its concern, its truly loving concern. To know this sort of experience is to be turned in the direction of salvation. It is, in fact, to be saved in the only meaningful way I know, for to be loved like this unconditionally is to be able to love; and to be so accepted is to be able to accept oneself and other people who possibly make little immediate appeal.

This secular salvation is initiated in a way sometimes not unlike religious conversion (the Damascus Road type), but more usually it grows out of an imperceptible response to a reality more intuitively known than consciously understood. I have witnessed lives transformed by something like love at first sight and, on the other hand, by the dawning recognition that one was loved for oneself alone to a degree previously thought impossible. Either way the whole exercise was redemptive and full of healing. That is atonement!

The same applies to our understanding of such crucial words as the incarnation, the transfiguration, the resurrection,[7] and so on. People who do not believe in anything like traditional terms order their lives on the intuitive assumption that the truths of incarnation, transfiguration, and resurrection are beyond dispute, the realities by which life finds its meaning and purpose. For instance, they do not believe in *the* incarnation, but they have no doubt about incarnation: the word – thought of in a variety of ways – becomes flesh time and again. They know the wonder of receiving sacrificial love and the glory of glimpsing beauty. In the innocence of a child they sometimes see into the heart of eternal values, and respond accordingly. Walking by the sea, climbing the hills, watching (as one man told me) an intricate piece of machinery, holding a new-born baby, loving and being loved, they suddenly feel – how shall I put it? – at peace with themselves and the whole world, caught up in an added dimension to life, gripped by reality that somehow points to a source beyond itself. Obviously they rarely think in these exact terms, but this is what they mean. They know the wonder of incarnation, of 'grace and truth' becoming flesh and dwelling among men.

Now the idea that Christ is anonymously present in the lives of everybody, believers and unbelievers alike, should not surprise readers of the New Testament. We are there told that: 'The real light (a reference to Jesus of Nazareth) which enlightens every man was even then coming into the world.' The reality of that Godlike element in all manner of people and often in the most surprising situations is irrefutable. What matters is how that spark can be fanned into a flame; how, in other words, Christ can be released within the self to do his saving work. It happens for some people within the existing structures of the church. The way of 'repent, believe, be born again', however interpreted, has yielded a rich harvest and set multitudes on the path of faith in the risen Christ.

What, though, of the others who do not think and function in such terms and yet whose lives bear witness that they are moving towards wholeness, growing in love and inner freedom? The only conclusion – indeed, the joyous conviction – to which we can come, that is, those of us who believe that Christ the Saviour *is* the 'light which enlightens every man',[8] is that secular man is learning new ways of liberating the indwelling presence in his life, new ways of opening the self to healing spiritual resources, new ways of co-operating with the 'hidden Christ' by paying attention, or perhaps more attention, to those areas of human experience which stand out as being crucial in his search for wholeness.

In such secular ways are men perceiving and feeling after ultimate meaning and purpose. Of course, we could insist that they will never find wholeness or become truly human until they join the institutional church and accept our theology. But this strikes me as being arrogantly over-simple to the point of near blasphemy.

NOTES

1. For some of the ideas of this chapter I gratefully acknowledge my indebtedness to the stimulus of John A. T. Robinson's 1970 Hulsean Lectures, to be published by SCM Press in 1973 under the title *The Human Face of God*.

2. Thomas J. Holmes, *Almost All are Welcome*, Lakeland Paperbacks 1970.

3. *The Listener*, 9 March 1972.

4. Monica Furlong, *Contemplating Now*, Hodder & Stoughton 1971, p.32.

5. Mark 9.24.

6. Anthony Storr, *The Integrity of the Personality*, Penguin Books 1970, p.37.

7. This is worked out in some detail in the next chapter.

8. John 1.9.

Life is Resurrection

Towards the end of his book *The Shaking of the Foundations*, Paul Tillich tells a remarkable story from the Nuremberg war-crime trials:

> A witness appeared who had lived for a time in a grave in a Jewish graveyard, in Wilna, Poland. It was the only place he – and many others – could live, when in hiding after they had escaped the gas chamber. During this time he wrote poetry, and one of the poems was a description of a birth. In a grave near by a young woman gave birth to a boy. The eighty-year-old gravedigger, wrapped in a linen shroud, assisted. When the newborn child uttered his first cry, the old man prayed: 'Great God, hast Thou finally sent the Messiah to us? For who else than the Messiah himself can be born in a grave?'[1]

That birth in a grave is symbolic of what in essence Christianity is all about. However, we shall never, I believe, get at the real-life meaning of resurrection, as distinct from believing in *the* resurrection, by arguing about whether or not Jesus of Nazareth did actually physically rise from the dead. Such matters are peripheral, if only because at the end of the day knowledge of resurrection power and glory is not dependent upon our believing that Jesus did indeed rise from the dead after the manner of the church's traditional teaching.

There are dedicated Christians for whom the physical resurrection of Christ is crucial to their faith. They assure me that if it could be proved that he did not rise bodily their Christianity would collapse and certainly in their eyes be discredited. I have no wish to persuade them to change their views or convictions. My concern is with the essential meaning of *the* resurrection for a growing number of people, inside as well as outside the institutional church, who find the traditional interpretation largely meaningless or superfluous. Are they, I want to ask, for ever cut off from the possibility of resurrection within themselves until they toe the line of orthodox belief? Or is such belief only one way of many of sharing the very real riches to which the word *resurrection* so clearly points?

Some Christian scholars have no hesitation about what to answer. 'So far as historicity is concerned,' wrote Ronald Gregor Smith, 'it is necessary to be plain: we may freely say that the bones of Jesus lie somewhere in Palestine.'[2] That comment, published in 1966, caused outrage in some circles and resulted in the commentator being written off as a 'safe' theologian. He was even called a heretic! What added to the confusion, and the significance of this cannot be overstressed, was that the people who knew Ronald Gregor Smith personally readily testified to the convincing evidence of resurrection in his own life. Whatever he thought about *the* resurrection he lived as one who kept company with the risen Lord. The paradox is surely worth pondering.

Though not identifying himself with Gregor Smith's extreme point of view, C. H. Dodd nevertheless corroborates the emphasis which the younger scholar was seeking to make. In his latest book, *The Founder of Christianity*, he wrote:

In describing occurrences which lay on the extreme edge of normal human experience, or beyond it, the writers (of the four gospels) are hardly pinned down to matter-of-fact precision in detail; and indeed the accounts they give, taken literally, are problematic if not contradictory. In various ways they are trying to justify, even to rationalize, what was for the original witnesses an immediate, intuitive certainty needing no justification. They were *dead sure* that they had met Jesus, and there was no more to be said about it.[3]

Now Ronald Gregor Smith was likewise *dead sure* that he had met Jesus – and, as I say, the people who knew him best were also *dead sure* that he had – but this clearly did not depend upon or necessitate his believing in the physical resurrection of Christ. He believed in resurrection for other reasons. This is not to say, let me make it abundantly clear, that belief in *the* resurrection is optional for the Christian, orthodox or otherwise. My concern at this point is simply to illustrate that differing interpretations of *the* resurrection, even fundamentally differing interpretations, do not appear to make any difference to experiential knowledge of its reality. In other words, the glories of resurrection life are not restricted to orthodox believers only: that is, believers who are orthodox at the moment.

After all, today's heresy is tomorrow's orthodoxy, as the history of Christian dogma makes clear. It was once orthodox, for instance, to believe in a three-decker universe with a flat earth; in the imminent return of Christ in the apostolic age; in the scientific accuracy of the Bible's creation stories; in man's salvation belonging exclusively to the institutional church; in the virgin birth as an indispensable article of faith; in hell fire for people outside the church; in the infallibility of the Pope's *ex cathedra* pronouncements; and in much else. But the lines of orthodoxy are no longer so clearly drawn and dogmatism is out of fashion. This is not because Christians have lost their conviction. It seems to me that they have never been more sure of their faith, but what they believe with the totality of their beings defies adequate or final articulation. *That* is the area of obscurity and the centre of uncertainty, which is another matter altogether from being unsure in any basic sense. Theology is about clues, not conclusions; and

Christians know in their very bones that they have enough clues about the meaning of life to justify their sometimes blind gropings for greater understanding of their faith.

Certainly this explains why I am a Christian. Some people call my beliefs orthodox; some not. But to me such considerations are unimportant. The vital matter is that the symbols of the birth, life, transfiguration, death and resurrection of Jesus speak to me of reality and meaning. They illuminate the inside of my experience of life from every standpoint. It concerns me little whether Jesus of Nazareth physically was raised from the dead; if his bones *were* found somewhere in Palestine it would not make a scrap of difference to my faith, the faith by which I function and understand life. For believing in him is for me a matter of knowing something of resurrection within myself – like new life in a grave – and discovering in terms which he suggests the pulsating and self-authenticating experience of old things passing away and all things becoming new. That is why I believe, and why countless Christians like me, aware of the ferment within the church of claim and counter claim, radicalism and reactionism, questioning conviction and lust for certainty, continue to follow the Christ of resurrection with unyielding assurance.

The four gospels make it plain that Jesus of Nazareth was preaching – and living! – his gospel of resurrection long before he rose from the dead. He acted, in other words, on the assumption that ultimate reality was love or – if that is not too clear – that the key to life was love, which, whatever the appearances to the contrary, always spoke the last word. This means that to do the loving thing, with its possible inescapable Gethsemane and cross, puts us on the side of life and resurrection, whereas to do the unloving thing allies us to death and its agencies. Love has within it the seeds of resurrection, and those seeds germinate and grow whenever love is at work. It does not matter whether such love is inspired by conscious belief in *the* resurrection or deliberate commitment to Jesus of Nazareth himself. Beyond doubt countless Christians are so inspired, but what finally matters most of all is the depth of the love, which clearly is not exclusive to Christianity. Likewise the spirit of forgiveness, reconciliation, creative goodness, disciplined freedom, the affirmation of personal value, and other qualities which Christ exemplified have within themselves, again whether defined in Christian terms or not, the seeds of resurrection. Wherever they operate signs of new life appear. To reduce such a fact of human experience to questions of theological debate, as though the latter somehow verified the former, is to turn the word made flesh into verbosity.

Unhappily, it is sometimes glaringly apparent that institutional religion is the enemy of new life. It was in the days of Jesus, and the history of the church, not to mention the record of other world religions, underlines how easily what was intended to facilitate *aliveness* does precisely the opposite. The letter of the law replaces the spirit, and principle becomes more important than people. No *one* is to blame. Usually the development happens imperceptibly as a whole community of believers, thinking of the church not only as an ambulance unit or a museum, but more particularly as a bulwark against change, fail to distinguish between defending the truth and living it. Almost invariably they are afraid of freedom, though the very idea provokes them to aggressive warnings against the arrogance of non-conformity.

On the other hand, institutional religion does frequently generate new life. There is no question about that. Within her structures signs of resurrection affirm the presence of the risen Lord and at the same time illustrate the intrinsic winsomeness, as well as rich variety, of such vitality. Wherever this is so, people are found whose approach to life is one of resurrection, inspired by their belief in *the* resurrection. However, it is obviously not just their claim to believe that makes them apostles and centres of new life. Numerous fellow-believers make the same claim, doubtless with sincerity, and remain as lifeless as ever. The essential requirement is the spirit of resurrection, with its characteristics of love, creative goodness, and so on, and this, as we have seen, is by no means dependent upon belief in *the* resurrection.

Multitudes of people, some of them surely known to us personally, live in the spirit of resurrection without necessarily believing in *the* resurrection. Such a comment is simply an appeal to human experience. I have no wish to argue, for your experience might be different from mine, but certainly I have known many people whose quality of life has led me irresistibly to the conclusion that though the gospel of Christ has its roots firmly wrapped round the rock of history our experience of resurrection, which is what the gospel is about, depends neither on our knowledge of those events nor our belief in them as formulated by the institutional church.

John V. Taylor, General Secretary of the Church Missionary Society, focuses the point I have in mind in one of his monthly newsletters. Telling the story of an African woman prisoner who was due to be transferred to a new open prison, he wrote:

> She knew that, if she made an escape, the woman officer who had pestered the authorities into making the experiment would be blamed, and the whole scheme might be abandoned. But she couldn't trust herself to observe the rules, so she begged to be put back behind bars. She was talked into sticking it out, until it slowly dawned on her that she was accepted as a normal, responsible person. For her, salvation came in this completely secular way, as it did to Zacchaeus. But all the ingredients of the salvation-experience were there as defined in classified theology:
>
> *Judgment* in her discovery that she preferred and actually belonged to the old life of high walls and hostility, rather than the new way of responsibility.
>
> *Repentance* in her desperately difficult turning-round towards

the new way and to the one who represented it and offered it to her.

Faith was the blind leap of trust, trusting another person's trust in her.

Forgiveness of sins was realized in the prison officer's confidence in her, without reference to her past unreliability. This was the new beginning, the clean sheet.

And the *cost of forgiveness* was there too: the officer who represented Christ to that woman placed herself and her career in that prisoner's hands, vulnerable and unreserved. That was the Cross in action, and it broke through the woman's pitiful lack of selfhood and brought something new to birth in her.

In that incident there took place something we can only describe as the transformation of the individual woman, and the beginnings of the transformation of the prison system of that country. Do we dare to say that it was not salvation? But in what sense was it a Christian experience?

Part of the answer lies in the fact that the patterns of the gospel experience are the patterns of life itself. The freedom and the protest of Jesus of Nazareth, his dying for us and his resurrection are both history and eternal reality. They happened, and they are the way things always happen. And we can be transformed, not only by relating to that past life and death and resurrection, in which the pattern was made plain once and for all, but also by relating to that true pattern wherever it emerges in the tissue of our contemporary experience.[4]

The resurrection of Christ *is* both history and eternal reality, which means that where the conditions of resurrection are being met new life is coming to birth. Let me provide actual examples of what I mean. Two widows, both as it happens orthodox Christians, were left with little children to bring up on severely limited incomes. They reacted in precisely opposite ways. One became resentful, self-pitying, critical of most things, fiercely independent, and a touchy crusader for righteousness of the joyless variety. The other, whose loneliness and suffering were no less pronounced, grew in stature and became more perceptive, compassionate, sensitive with a capacity for empathy that at times was awe-inspiring, and somehow unhurried in her busyness. Most impressive of all was her strong gentleness.

The same experience detracted from one woman and yet released new life in the other. Clearly the explanation was other than their belief in *the* resurrection, a belief they both declared with conviction and undoubted sincerity. What happened was that one of them faced the calamity of her unexpected situation, accepted it in the sense of deliberately absorbing it, and far from trying to run away or fighting what could not be changed chose to co-operate with what life had done to her. She realized, I suppose, that it is not what life does to us, but what we do with life when it does it, which is the crucial factor.

Whatever the explanation, with heavy heart she picked up the fragments that remained *that nothing be lost*. In other words she 'listened' to what life was saying to her in the tragedy and slowly moved in the direction of response. It was not easy, but healing came, assuring her and the people nearest to her that resurrection – the forces of life seeking to defeat the decay of death, hope rising from the ruins of near despair, healing flowing into wounds of separation and aloneness – was living experience now; that the death she died deep within herself at her husband's departure was incredibly the herald of resurrection.

I saw the same surge of new life in a situation of shock and fear. A young couple had been looking forward to the birth of their first child, and the event itself, with the husband present, had fulfilled their highest hopes. The baby, a girl, was sturdy and well, the object of their love and symbolic of even deeper feelings that now bound them together. Three or four days later the husband was called aside by a doctor. Worst fears were confirmed, he explained. The baby was a mongol.

Grey-faced and anxious for his wife, the husband gently told her the news. They wept together. He simply said, 'We shall have to love her all the more.' They did, too, if that were possible. I watched the miracle happen. What could have shattered the marriage and turned the man and his wife into cynics wallowing in bitterness became instead a means of resurrection. The young couple, their eyes wide open, totally accepted the situation. New life emerged from the grave of initial despair. This is not to say that the way was easy. It included its Gethsemanes and Golgothas, and *compelled* the two concerned to carry a cross they never expected. But the spirit with which they lived through the early part of the experience was so conducive to new life that it turned every intimation of distress and death into hope and a promise of creation. Beyond their awareness they witnessed to the invulnerability of love and the nature of its triumph. As an observer, involved by nothing more than my natural sympathy, I came to believe in the message of the empty tomb, to believe it with another dimension to my thinking altogether. It doesn't seem to me important how *the* resurrection happened. The fact is, I have no doubt, that the Lord of resurrection is alive in the world. I met him in that young couple and their mongol baby.

This sort of experience surely comes to us all, sooner or later, though probably we articulate it in a variety of ways. But when it does words tend to get in the way and lead to arguments about secondary matters. The reason is that resurrection is an experience before it is a doctrine and is affirmed by a man's whole personality, not just his mind. I remember sitting by the bedside of a middle-aged woman who was dying of leukaemia. I knew her well for many years. She was a churchless saint. By that I mean simply that she never practised religion as conventionally observed; she did not believe in the God of institutional religion and never went to

church. Yet her own life was an expression of creative goodness. The very idea would have amused and, I think, puzzled
her, but she was in fact the incarnation of love. I have known a
number of saints (people whose spirit was reminiscent of
Jesus of Nazareth), but not one of them was more loving or
self-forgetful than this woman. Even as she died she was
concerned about the people nearest to her. And it was not the
concern of fussiness, the sort that modestly calls attention to
itself and the supposed indispensable service it represents.
She really cared without self-consciousness or pretentiousness
of any kind.

As I reflected on her life I saw vividly once more that her
capacity for love was the measure of her quiet vivacity. With
little to commend her in terms of outstanding achievements,
the sort of person few people would notice in a crowd, she was
nevertheless very much *alive*. Within the love she sustained
there were seeds of resurrection which time and again took
root in situations of suffering and adversity. The spirit in
which she lived made her one of the most profoundly religious
persons of my experience. She did not believe – or disbelieve
for that matter – in *the* resurrection; she lived it.

This doubtless explained my thoughts and feelings as I sat
by her bed. And when I heard shortly afterwards that she was
dead I was first of all angry and then unbelieving; angry because
it seemed almost indecent that such a lovely person should
suffer so much and die the victim of a cruel disease, and
unbelieving because I could not accept that death was stronger
than her love or that all the lovely potential she represented
was no longer capable of fulfilment. Such considerations apart,
I know that in her presence I was conscious of a presence
other than the pair of us; and that to describe her life I need
the symbolism of Jesus of Nazareth – his birth, life, death and
resurrection. For only that sort of meaning is adequate. Other
people, I realize, not sharing my faith in him, would use

other terms and symbols, but fundamentally, I believe, we would be talking about the same reality of resurrection, the irrepressible surge of life, of new creation, that becomes a part of human experience whenever love is allowed to do its healing work.

On another plane altogether, this same awareness that 'the patterns of the gospel experience are the patterns of life itself' apprehended a group of British soldiers in a Japanese prisoner-of-war camp during the Second World War. Recalling the experience, Laurens van der Post wrote:

> It was amazing how often my men would confess to me, that for the first time in their lives they had realized the truth, and the dynamic liberating power of the first of the Crucifixion utterances, 'Forgive them for they know not what they do'. I found that the moment they grasped this fundamental fact of our prison situation, forgiveness became a project not of an act of will or of personal virtue even, but an automatic and all-compelling consequence of a law of understanding: as real and indestructible as Newton's law of gravity . . . Forgiveness, my prison experience had taught me, was not mere religious sentimentality; it was as fundamental a law of the human spirit as the law of gravity. If one broke the law of gravity one broke one's neck; if one broke this law of forgiveness one inflicted a mortal wound on one's spirit and became once again a member of the chain-gang of mere cause and effect from which life has laboured so long and painfully to escape.[5]

British soldiers are usually neither fervent churchgoers nor well versed in Christian theology, but clearly this did not prevent them from experiencing what I have called resurrection life at the point of probably their greatest vulnerability to hate and alienation. Their attitude of forgiveness, unrelated to any conscious faith in God or the church's ministry of grace, not only fostered the spirit of reconciliation, but introduced into their situation a new factor, one that challenged all the life-denying forces both around them and within them. They perceived that the law of forgiveness, like the law of gravity, is the way life works. And as in John V. Taylor's story of the new prison, this particular prisoner-of-war camp illustrates that all the ingredients of the biblical salvation-experience are sometimes found in the most secular of settings. These British tommies did not think of themselves in New Testament terms at all; the very idea would probably have evoked expletives of derision and possible embarrassment. But who can doubt that they knew from the inside the truths with which the four gospels are notably concerned: penitence, forgiveness, turning the other cheek, initiating reconciliation, meeting rejection with acceptance, and hate with compassion. I have no wish to claim more than the experience warrants, for doubtless not all the men felt the same, and those who did were not consistent in their attitude to the 'enemy', but Laurens van der Post's words are, I believe, justification enough for my observation that people live in the spirit of the Christian gospel without consciously believing it. For a variety of reasons, not least the church's influence in the world for almost 2,000 years, they adopt an attitude to life which reflects the outlook of Jesus of Nazareth. The result is that the patterns of his gospel become the patterns of their living. In functional terms they dwell within the revelation he brought into the world and thereby discover the truth that sets men free. The fact that they attribute their freedom to an 'all-compelling consequence of a law of understanding: as real and indestructible as Newton's law of gravity' in no way invalidates the freedom or changes the truth of which Jesus of Nazareth is the revelation in history. It simply means that they are appropriating the insights of that revelation – perhaps imbibing is a better word – in ways personal to themselves but no less effectual in introducing them to experiences of resurrection.

This is movingly illustrated by, of all men, Thomas Henry Huxley, an agnostic who indeed coined the word to describe his attitude to religion. He had a favourite son who died young, and a few days after his body had been put into the earth he wrote to the Rev. Charles Kingsley. The date was September, 1860.

As I stood behind the coffin of my little son the other day, with my mind bent on anything but disputation, the officiating minister read, as a part of his duty, the words 'If the dead rise not again, let us eat and drink, for tomorrow we die.' I cannot tell you how inexpressibly they shocked me. St Paul had neither wife nor child, or he must have known that his alternative involved a blasphemy against all that was best and noblest in human nature. I could have laughed with scorn. What! Because I am face to face with irreparable loss, because I have given back to the source from whence it came, the cause of a great happiness, still retaining through all my life the blessings which have sprung and will spring from that cause, I am to renounce my manhood, and, howling, grovel in bestiality? Why, the very apes know better, and if you shoot their young, the poor brutes grieve their grief out and do not immediately seek distraction in a gorge.

Kicked into the world, a boy without guide or training, or with worse than none, I confess to my shame that few men have drunk deeper of all kinds of sin than I. Happily, my course was arrested in time – before I earned absolute destruction – and for long years I have been slowly and painfully climbing, with many a fall, towards better things. And when I look back, what do I find to have been the agents of my redemption? The hope of immortality or of future reward? I can honestly say that for these fourteen years such a consideration has not entered my head. No, I can tell you exactly what has been at work. Sartor Resartus led me to know that a deep sense of religion was compatible with the entire absence of theology. Secondly, science and her methods gave me a resting-place independent of authority and tradition. Thirdly, love opened up to me a view of the sanctity of human nature, and impressed me with a deep sense of responsibility.

If in the supreme moment when I looked into my boy's grave my sorrow was full of submission and without bitterness, it is because these agencies have worked upon me, and not because I have ever cared whether my poor personality shall remain for ever from the All from whence it came and whither it goes.

And thus, my dear Kingsley, you will understand what my position is. I may be quite wrong, and in that case I know I shall have to pay the penalty for being wrong. But I can only say with Luther, 'Gott helfe mir, Ich kann nichts anders.' 'God help me, I can do no other.'[6]

I know of few more 'religious' documents. It is true that Thomas Henry Huxley did not believe the church's teaching, but who can doubt, in the light of this letter, that he knew plenty about resurrection! He was sceptical about *the* resurrection and found himself unable to accept the idea of immortality, but the dimension to life to which both articles of faith point he surely knew *as present experience*. And it is to that experience that Jesus of Nazareth calls us, some through membership of the church, some by another route. Each of us must find that way for himself, and we shall know that we are moving in the right direction by one infallible sign – the degree to which we are *alive*. For in the final analysis the gospel of Christ is about resurrection, which means that only as new creation begins to emerge in the graveyard within ourselves can we be sure that we are in the presence of the risen Lord. For he is the Lord of *life*!

NOTES

1. Paul Tillich, *The Shaking of the Foundations*, SCM Press 1949; Penguin Books 1962, pp.166–7.

2. Ronald Gregor Smith, *Secular Christianity*, Collins 1966, p.103.

3. C. H. Dodd, *The Founder of Christianity*, Collins 1971, p.170.

4. *CMS news-letter*, September 1969.

5. Laurens van der Post, *The Night of the New Moon*, Hogarth Press 1970, p.154.

6. Leonard Huxley, *Life and Letters of Thomas Henry Huxley*, Gregg International 1970, Vol. 1, p.220.